TRANSFORMING POWER OF TECHNOLOGY

TRANSFORMING POWER OF TECHNOLOGY

THE **INTERNET**

Sandra Weber

CHELSEA HOUSE
P U B L I S H E R S
A Haights Cross Communications Company

Philadelphia

Frontis: With the explosion of the Internet, numerous cyber cafés have opened up, becoming popular destinations for people who want to talk, drink, and access the World Wide Web.

CHELSEA HOUSE PUBLISHERS

VP, NEW PRODUCT DEVELOPMENT Sally Cheney
DIRECTOR OF PRODUCTION Kim Shinners
CREATIVE MANAGER Takeshi Takahashi
MANUFACTURING MANAGER Diann Grasse

Staff for THE INTERNET

EXECUTIVE EDITOR Lee Marcott
ASSOCIATE EDITOR Kate Sullivan
PRODUCTION ASSISTANT Megan Emery
PICTURE RESEARCHER Amy Dunleavy
SERIES AND COVER DESIGNER Keith Trego
LAYOUT 21st Century Publishing and Communications Inc.

http://www.chelseahouse.com

First Printing

1 3 5 7 9 8 6 4 2

Library of Congress Cataloging-in-Publication Data applied for.

ISBN 0-7910-7449-8

CONTENTS

1 Life in Cyberspace

AT ISSUE

At the start of the 1990s, just a few computer buffs used the Internet. The World Wide Web had just been invented. People shopped in malls and watched television for entertainment. They read about world events only in daily newspapers and used telephones and postal services to communicate with relatives across the country. By the year 2000, half of all Americans used the Internet. With the click of a mouse, Internet users could explore the world, unencumbered by space, time, or telephone tariffs.

"It's no wonder so many people compared the 1990s Internet to the psychedelic 1960s," writes journalist Douglas Rushkoff. "It seemed all we needed to do was get a person online, and he or she would be changed forever. And people were. A 60-year-old Midwestern businessman I know found himself logging on every night to engage in a conversation about Jungian archetypes. It lasted for four weeks before he realized the person with whom he was conversing was a 16-year-old boy from Tokyo."[1]

WHERE DID YOU GO TODAY?

More than half the U.S. population now has access to the Internet at home, the office, or school. "The Internet is entering the mainstream of American society," states Lutz Erbring, coauthor of a Stanford University study on the Internet and society.[2] The Internet is a growing part of our lives and there is no turning back.

In 2000, there were about 200 million Internet users, and by

Young people between the ages of 2 and 17 are among the most savvy Internet users. More than half of them connect from home for help with homework as well as to surf the Web, play games, and e-mail friends.

early 2001, there were over 400 million. Kids are a big part of this trend. Among young people ages 2 to 17, over 50 percent are connected to the Internet at home. "Everybody is going to be a user soon," says Norman H. Nie, coauthor of the Stanford study. "That means we can expect to see large changes for communities and society as a whole."[3]

People now expect other people and institutions to be online. Access is taken almost for granted. Exchanging e-mail is a great way to stay in touch with friends and family. Sometimes, students take classes online, not in a physical building. People often work by telecommuting and shoppers surf the Web instead of strolling at the mall. Friends around the world play Internet games and swap music. The average user spent over 20 hours looking at Internet sites during March 2001.

The Internet was not intended to be a mass medium for interpersonal communication. It was built and funded mostly by the U.S. Department of Defense to allow scientists to run programs on remote computers. Yet from almost the beginning, users had other ideas. Janet Abbate admits that as a computer programmer in the mid-1980s, she knew the Internet was for scientific research, but chatting with friends and swapping recipes with strangers was also part of her day. "Rather like taking a tank for a joyride!" she writes.[4]

Another early adopter of the Internet, Brendan P. Kehoe, wrote a manual in 1992 to tell new users how to operate this "great new Internet link." In the preface of *Zen and the Art of the Internet*, he warned users: "This territory we are entering can become a fantastic time-sink. Hours can slip by, people can come and go, and you'll be locked into Cyberspace."[5]

Because it runs 24 hours a day, seven days a week, the Internet transforms the concept of time. It redefines the limits of work time and play time. Now people can work, shop, talk, learn, and entertain themselves online any time, and for as long as they want—since Internet service providers now charge a flat fee rather than a per-minute price. Web pages change on a daily, if not hourly, basis. Many sites actually run in real time, delivering messages and data immediately. On the Internet, it's often said, "five minutes ago is old news."

The seemingly endless expanse of cyberspace offers a smorgasbord of opportunities and activities. Every day new functions, new resources, and new possibilities arise on the Internet.

Eighteen-year-old Becky Juarez could not imagine life without the Internet. She enjoyed gossiping about her favorite movie stars, socializing in chat rooms, and discovering information about the college she would attend. Then she discovered a whole new world: websites in her native language, Spanish. The number of Web pages in Spanish is growing faster than the number of pages in English.

The Internet helps Ralph Senst, 46, an International Business Machines Corp. (IBM) vice president, oversee 3,000 workers, 300 of them researchers, from a small office in his Victorian home in a suburb of Chicago. He ventures downtown to his office in a high-rise building only twice a month.

Lots of people use the Internet to research their family tree. Staff at New York's Ellis Island American Family Immigration History Center and the Mormon Church are working together to create a database containing the arrival records of 22 million immigrants who came through the port between 1892 and 1924. This database is available to anyone via the Internet at *http://www.ellisislandrecords.org.*

Many organizations reevaluated their communication avenues and started using websites and e-mail. In 1993, the White House went online and provided e-mail addresses for the president, vice president, and first lady. The site called Operation Homefront went online two years later. It provides a way for American service-people stationed abroad to communicate with their families and supporters. The Internal Revenue Service (IRS) uses a website to distribute tax forms and information about the tax code.

Even the Vatican started to use the Internet to get out their message. In 1995, Pope John Paul II presided over the creation of a Vatican website. In his message on World Communications Day 2002, the pope said, "For the Church, the new world of cyberspace is a summons to the great adventure of using its potential to proclaim the Gospel message. . . . With those opportunities come risks, however, including the Internet's well-known ability to spread 'degrading and damaging [material].'" [6]

At the United Nations, Secretary-General Kofi Annan is deter-mined to put the Internet to good use. Annan has proposed an Internet health network that will provide state-of-the-art medical knowledge to 10,000 clinics and hospitals in poor countries.

In the United States, several pages that emerged on the World Wide Web hours after the 1995 Oklahoma City bombing documented the destruction and offered help and support to those in need. While rumors often blurred together with the facts, one thing was clear: the Internet had become a prime source of breaking news.

Pope John Paul II has harnessed the power of the Internet to communicate with the public and clergy around the world. In 1995, he inaugurated a Vatican website, and he is shown here in 2001 sending — for the first time in the history of the Catholic Church — an official pontifical document to bishops over the Internet.

The Internet was the only means of communication between survivors of the 1995 Kobe earthquake in Japan and their family and friends around the world. Amateur news correspondents kept the news moving. Some of the correspondents were actually in the city, while others were transmitting images from Japanese television onto the Internet.

The first rumor of President Bill Clinton's sexual relationship with former White House intern Monica Lewinsky was reported on the Drudge Report website. Users scrambled to get online for more information. There were more visits to media websites in the week after the story broke than at any time in the

Web's history. When Independent Counsel Kenneth Starr released his findings about Clinton and Lewinsky to the Web on September 11, 1998, millions of people raced to download the 445-page report. The enormous demand crashed the Internet, temporarily bringing communications to a halt.

Three years later, on the morning of September 11, 2001, the Internet carried earth-shattering news of terrorist attacks in the United States. The surge of users trying to get breaking news slowed network response time. In the following 48 hours, more than 4 million people used the Internet. They contacted family and friends by e-mail and searched the Internet for information on what had happened. Although the Internet was of great help to people during this tragic time, government investigators later indicated that e-mail had also helped the perpetrators communicate and organize the attacks.

Clearly, the Internet has reached all corners of the world and is being used both for good and for bad purposes. It has removed geographic barriers and reconfigured human communities. According to one observer, "Core economic, social, political, and cultural activities throughout the planet are being structured by and around the Internet, and other computer networks."[7]

A NETWORK OF NETWORKS

The Internet is a worldwide connection of thousands of networks linking millions of computers. The term Internet means *Inter*connected *Net*work. In essence, the Internet is a network of networks.

It is the agreement of all of these computer networks to follow the same communications rules that makes the Internet's many networks work together as a seemingly harmonious entity. The formal name of those rules, collectively called a protocol, is Transmission Control Protocol/Internet Protocol (TCP/IP). All of the networks and computers connected to the Internet must recognize TCP/IP. (A network that uses TCP/IP but is accessible only to people within an organization is called an intranet.)

Most of the Internet traffic is handled by the backbones. A backbone is a system of routers and other transmission equipment (cables, wires, and wireless links) that handles the connections between the computer networks. The majority of at-home users connect through ordinary phone lines, high-speed digital phone lines, superfast coaxial cable, or satellite dishes to an Internet Service Provider (ISP), which connects to a backbone. Another option is to become a member of an information service like

America Online (AOL)

Steve Case had a notion in 1989 that lots of mainstream people were really interested in online services, but did not really know much about computers. So, he created America Online (AOL), a commercial online service that held the novice's hand and introduced hoards of users to the online world. For a monthly fee, subscribers have access to news, chat rooms, shopping, e-mail, and a multitude of other features, some available exclusively from that information service.

Contrary to popular belief, AOL is not part of the Internet. For the first few years of its existence, AOL competed with the Internet and refused to offer a way for its customers to connect to it. Today, AOL is the world's largest Internet service provider, with 35 million members.

AOL is known for pioneering such technologies as using keywords for simple navigation and the Buddy List feature that enables instant messaging by displaying the IDs of members' buddies who are online. AOL also has built-in parental control tools that help parents protect their children from inappropriate materials.

At times, AOL's service was slow and gave people a poor impression of the Internet. For e-commerce vendors, AOL's problems limited the number of customers visiting their shops. But AOL continued to grow, and in January 2000 it announced its merger with the Time Warner film, magazine, and cable TV empire.

AOL stock shares were valued at $72 at the time of the merger. But, like other high-tech companies, it took a nosedive and in October 2002, the stock was worth just $12. AOL users remain extremely loyal, however, with 79 percent of 2000 members still subscribers in 2001.

America Online (AOL), which provides an Internet connection in addition to features only available to AOL members.

When users connected to the Internet in the late 1980s, they primarily used electronic mail (e-mail), telnet, and File Transfer Protocol (FTP). These three functions were the foundation of the Internet for many years. Today, however, the Internet provides a multitude of services.

E-mail is the most widely used capability of the Internet.

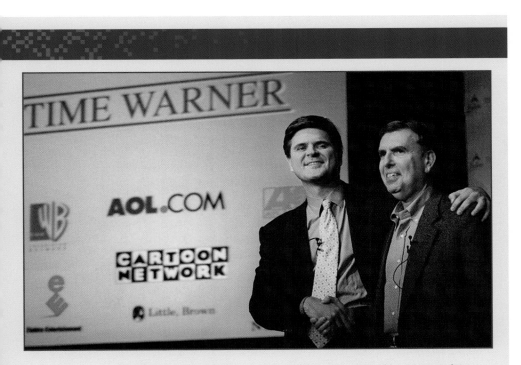

Chairmen and chief executives of their respective companies, Steve Case of America Online, left, and Gerald Levin of Time Warner, announced in January 2000 that the Internet service provider and media giant would merge. AOL, with 35 million loyal members, is the world's largest Internet service provider.

At first, e-mail handled only plain text, but now pictures, sound, and even video can be included in a message. With one click of a mouse, e-mail is sent to a friend across the street or to a group of 10,000 people spread all over the world. Incoming mail queues up in an In Box and can be read at any time. The user can respond to, forward, file, or delete the message.

Telnet is used to access a computer system across town or around the globe. A PC acts as if it is a terminal linked directly to a host computer. A user can log on, usually as an anonymous user, and then run programs, search databases, or perform other tasks on the remote computer.

The FTP application allows files to be transferred over the Internet. Files containing data such as software programs, music, or IRS tax forms can be uploaded (sent to the Internet) and downloaded (copied from the Internet) using FTP.

Bulletin boards, e-mail lists (listservs), Usenet, and similar services allow users to share information about their interests, such as skateboarding, farming, or stamp collecting. Internet Relay Chat (IRC) allows people to communicate in real time. As users type at their keyboards, the text is seen almost instantaneously by people in the chat room.

Gopher provides a menu-based interface to resources on the Internet, such as weather data, maps, and technical reports. Users navigate through menus to locate the text, pictures, or information they need. Gopher fell out of favor after the World Wide Web became popular.

The World Wide Web is the Internet's most powerful and revolutionary application. It is a collection of documents, or Web pages, that can be easily accessed by clicking on hyperlinks within other pages. A Web browser such as Netscape Communicator or Microsoft Explorer is the interface to Web resources and, more recently, provides a way to use other services such as e-mail, FTP, and telnet.

Because the Web is their only contact with the Internet, many users think the Web and the Internet are interchangeable, but they are not. The Internet is made of physical computers and cables whereas the World Wide Web is an application that runs on the Internet. Tim Berners-Lee, inventor of the Web, explains:

> On the Net, the connections are cables between computers; on the Web, connections are hypertext links. The Web exists because of programs which communicate between computers on the Net. The Web could not be without the Net. The Web made the Net useful because people are really interested in information (not to mention knowledge and wisdom!) and don't really want to have to know about computers and cables.[8]

THE POWER OF COMMUNICATION

The Internet is primarily used as a communication medium. It provides a way for people and organizations to receive information. However, unlike television, radio, and the newspaper, which are passive media, the Internet lets the audience instantly respond to what they see and hear. Online purchase forms take orders, for example, and prompts solicit actions. More significantly, e-mail and the Web allow people to create content and publish it for viewing by friends, coworkers, and curious onlookers.

Another powerful characteristic of Internet communications is that they can be one-to-one (by sending an e-mail) or one-to-many (by sending e-mail to multiple recipients, chatting, or posting a Web page). On the whole, the Internet is many-to-many because many people speak to many other people. Companies, nations, and communities are no longer restricted to a physical grouping of people.

In their analysis of the twentieth century, Peter Jennings and Todd Brewster wrote:

> The Internet played a big part in making the world seem smaller. People could now communicate with each other around the world, instantly, without laws or controls or many

government restrictions. Many believed that the computer and the fax machine were vital to the collapse of Communism. A system that depended on controlling information simply could not withstand the new technologies. All people needed for ideas and information to flow was a computer and a phone line.[9]

Dissidents use the Internet to evade censorship of their messages, musicians put their music on the Web for fans to download, and "day traders" buy stocks online with the click of a mouse. "It is not just a change in how we compute or communicate," writes Andrew L. Shapiro in *The Control Revolution*. "Rather,

Fact, Fluff, or Fraud

There is no doubt that the Internet is a powerful research tool. However, because anyone is free to publish anything, users must think critically about the information they access on the Internet. A snazzy website is so simple to create that a ten-year-old can do it. The information does not have to pass through a content review by experts or fact checking by editors or spell checking by proofreaders. Anyone can write and post information on bicycle repair, Roman history, nail polish, or brain surgery. But some so-called facts or advice might be a lie, hoax, or sales pitch.

Sorting the valid information from the inaccurate and the deceptive is necessary, but may be difficult. Start by thinking about who created the information. Are names and credentials provided on the site? Try to determine if the hosts of a site are experts.

Look at the website address, or URL. Consider why this person or organization might be presenting the information. Are they trying to sell something? Do they have a hidden agenda? Does the information differ from your current knowledge? Checking other sources may clarify any controversy that arises.

Investigate when the page was created and when the information was last updated. Also, look at the links they post to other pages to see if you can verify the information.

it is a potentially radical shift in who is in *control*—of information, experience, and resources. . . . [N]ew technology is allowing individuals to take power from large institutions such as government, corporations, and the media." [10]

Individuals have the power to bypass record companies, stockbrokers, and censors. They can force corporate executives and politicians to respond to issues of concern. The Web allows us to publish news, sell products, compare products, find information, and have global conversations. The Internet expands individuals' power to communicate.

Amid all the enthusiasm for the Internet, however, there is also a feeling of uneasiness. Some people actually feel they lack control because of the technology. They fear the Internet will dominate their lives. Others wonder about its effect on employment, education, social protection, and lifestyle. Will it destroy our privacy and corrupt children? Will the creation of virtual worlds make people care less about the real world?

Others ask: Will the Internet enlighten people of different cultures? Can it bring freedom and equality to the world?

The Internet is not a toxic concoction, nor is it a magic potion. It is a tool that can be used in many different ways—some good, some bad. To consider the implications of the Internet on society, it is helpful to look at how the Internet developed and how it is controlled. By further studying its influence on various aspects of society, an understanding of the nature, power, and limitations of this technology can be achieved.

Anthony Rutkowski, former executive director of the Internet Society, said: "A hundred years from now, history may well record the emergence and implementation of the Internet protocol as a profound turning point in the evolution of human communication—of much greater significance than the creation of the printing press." [11]

2

The Roots of the Internet

The Internet was once compared to England's famous Stonehenge, the huge, 50-ton stone blocks assembled around 1600 B.C., possibly to function as an astronomical device and calculator. "Like Stonehenge, the Internet taken as a whole may seem a daunting and complex thing," wrote Vinton G. Cerf, one of pioneers of the Internet. "It is hard to imagine how something as large and complex could be designed, built and made to work at all. But, also like Stonehenge, the Internet was not built all at once, but in phases. Its size and complexity evolved over time." [12]

Building the Internet involved government, industry, and academia working as partners in creating and developing a new technology. Many talented, dedicated, and selfless individuals worked on this collaboration. No one person or single organization invented the Internet.

Without this vision of cooperation, innovation, and freedom, what would the Internet look like today? Can the cooperative spirit continue as the Internet grows and diverse forces seek to gain control and amass wealth by their use of it?

HOW DID IT START?

The beginning of the Internet was sparked when the USSR launched *Sputnik*, the first space satellite to orbit Earth, on October 10, 1957. "*Sputnik* surprised the nation and the world. [President] Eisenhower told the secretary of defense, 'I don't want to be surprised like this again, the nation shouldn't be surprised like this again.' So they wanted an agency created

The 1957 takeoff of the Soviet spacecraft *Sputnik* launched not only the first satellite to orbit the Earth and the space race, but also the Internet. President Dwight D. Eisenhower established the Advanced Research Projects Agency in an effort to close the gap between Soviet and American technology. ARPA developed ARPANET, the precursor to the Internet, to permit high-tech researchers and the Department of Defense to share data.

to fund especially promising high technology," recalls Bob Taylor, who would later work for that agency, the Advanced Research Projects Agency (ARPA).[13]

As ARPA began its work, the ongoing cold war between the Soviets and the Americans was in the public consciousness. An American U-2 spy plane was shot down over the USSR in 1960. The Berlin Wall went up in 1961. The Cuban Missile Crisis occurred in 1962. It seemed urgent that the U.S. government catch up with the technology of the Soviet Union.

At that time, computers were large, expensive, and scarce. University professors, science researchers, and government specialists used these big mainframe computers to manipulate large sets of numbers. One of ARPA's main goals was to set up communications between the country's leading scientists and the Department of Defense.

Sharing data or software between computers usually meant a person had to physically carry a reel of magnetic tape or a stack of punch cards from one machine to the other. A scientist who needed to use a distant computer usually got on a plane and flew to the machine. Modems, which allowed computers to send data over a phone line, had been introduced in the late 1950s, but setting up a telephone connection between two computers was expensive and error-prone. The other problem with sharing information between computers was that not all machines used the same software programs. They could not communicate directly with each other.

A small group of computer scientists envisioned how computers might be linked together to allow one computer to talk to another, thus allowing researchers to share data across the country. Like other inventors in technology, they were driven by a desire for easier and more reliable long-range communications and by an urge to explore new frontiers.

One scientist with that vision was Taylor, head of research and development for ARPA at the Pentagon and the man who can most truly claim global computer networking as his brainchild. "Computers were first born as arithmetic engines," said Taylor, "but my own view, and the view of some other people as well, is that they're much more interesting and powerful as communication devices because they mediate human-to-human communication." [14]

The team of computer scientists and researchers at ARPA envisioned a huge "galactic network" of computers. Of course, in 1968 there were only a few thousand computers in the country. "As I think back, I really do believe I was thinking about all the machines in the world," recalls Larry Roberts, a Massachusetts Institute of Technology (MIT) researcher who joined the ARPA project. "I don't think we thought that there were going to be that many." [15]

THE JOURNEY FROM ARPANET TO INTERNET

On July 20, 1969, American Neil Armstrong stepped out of the lunar module *Eagle* and walked on the moon. The success of the *Apollo 11* mission gave U.S. citizens something to feel good about in the space race. That same year, the government's computer networking program took a giant leap, too. The vision of a galactic network took shape.

ARPA contracted with the small Cambridge, Massachusetts, firm of Bolt, Beranek, and Newman (BBN) to build the first Interface Message Processors (IMPs) for the network. BBN delivered the first IMP to the University of California at Los Angeles (UCLA) in September. The next month, the second IMP was installed at Stanford Research Institute, and researchers sent the first message from UCLA to Stanford. No one recorded the message or announced it to the press. No one had realized the historical significance of the event.

By the end of 1969, these two computers, along with one at the University of Utah and another at the University of California at Santa Barbara, formed the initial network called ARPANET. This tiny network eventually spanned the entire world and was the precursor to the Internet.

In 1969, Neil Armstrong became the first man to walk on the moon, and the United States become more confident in its technology. Advances in building the Internet paralleled the country's success in the space race. The same year as Armstrong's historic first steps, ARPANET became the first computer network to connect two research institutions — the University of California at Los Angeles and the Stanford Research Institute in Menlo Park.

The method of communication within the network was based on packet-switching technology. This technology had tremendous impact on the capabilities and composition of the present-day Internet. Donald Davies of Great Britain outlined the concept and was the first to use the word "packets."

Unaware of Davies' work, Paul Baran of the Rand Corporation independently developed the same concept. Baran originally referred to it as "hot potato routing," since it resembled how a hot potato is juggled from hand to hand. In a similar way, messages are broken into parts (packets) and the packets are routed from system to system toward their destination and then reassembled and delivered to the recipient. Each packet may take very different geographic paths.

Baran's work was part of the Rand Corporation's efforts to find a way to link the government's computers so that they could communicate even after a nuclear attack. Baran reasoned that a central authority would be vulnerable to being destroyed, but if power and control were decentralized, then the network could function even if some parts of it were destroyed. All computers on the network would have equal ability to communicate with other computers and messages could be passed through the network by any number of paths to their destination. Thus, if some computers on the network failed, messages would simply be routed by another path.

Because of Baran's work with defense applications, a myth circulated that the Internet was created to survive a nuclear war. Even though it was not true, it was a good story and was even printed in *Time* magazine. Bob Taylor, ARPANET's originator, recalled: "*Time* said the ARPANET was built to enable Defense Department scientists to connect to one another in the event of a nuclear war. I wrote a letter to *Time* pointing out they were mistaken, and they wrote a letter back to me assuring me that their sources were correct."[16]

By the end of 1971, ARPANET consisted of about 24 computers at sites including MIT and Harvard University. In

1973, University College in London and the Royal Radar Establishment in Norway became the first international connections to ARPANET. The network grew quickly, and by 1974 it included 62 sites. By 1981, there were more than 200 sites.

Concern about "intrusion by unauthorized, possibly malicious, users" caused the U.S. military to break off its users from ARPANET and form MILNET in 1983.[17] University and research networks remained connected to ARPANET. In 1986, the National Science Foundation (NSF) launched NSFNET, which linked five U.S. supercomputing centers. The following year, NSF took over the funding and management of a large portion of what was being called the Internet.

ARPANET had served its purpose and was shut down in 1989. ARPANET pioneer Vinton Cerf looked back with fondness at the legendary network and wrote "Requiem for the ARPANET." It ends:

> Now pause with me a moment, shed some tears.
>
> For auld lang syne, for love, for years and years
>
> of faithful service, duly done, I weep.
>
> Lay down thy packet, now, O friend, and sleep.[18]

In that same year, the Berlin Wall separating West Berlin from East Germany was torn down. Communist regimes throughout the world collapsed and the cold war ended.

The Internet expanded, and on May 1, 1995, the NSF handed over its responsibility for the Internet's main backbone to private businesses such as IBM, AT&T, and GTE. By that time, over 90 countries had direct connections to the Internet, and links to other worldwide networks reached 168 countries.

"It's a bit like climbing a mountain," said Cerf. "You don't know how far you've come until you stop and look back."[19]

SPINNING THE WEB

In the 1960s, 1970s, and 1980s, the Internet was hard to use. A small group of scientists had mastered the cryptic Internet commands, but businesspeople had no interest in learning commands for a system that they thought had no foreseeable potential. They left the Internet to the so-called nerds. That was fine with the nerds; they did not want the network to be used commercially.

The harmonious accord did not last long. Internet commands began to get easier and a few nontechnical people began to use the Internet. Libraries began to automate card catalogues and make them available online via telnet. Users created applications such as ARCHIE (an archiver for FTP) and WAIS (Wide Area Information Server), which indexed sites and made finding information among the multitude of sites much easier. In 1972, e-mail was introduced, and that caught people's attention.

Bob Kahn, who was part of the team that built the IMPs for ARPANET, recognized that people were not astounded by the resource-sharing capability of the network. "You know, everyone really uses this thing for electronic mail," he said to a colleague.[20]

By the 1990s, the Internet no longer belonged to the nerds. Business executives, schoolchildren, politicians, artists, housewives, and people from every corner of society jumped online. Three innovations brought the Internet to mainstream America: Gopher, the World Wide Web, and Navigator.

A friendly GUI (graphical user interface) for the Internet called Gopher was developed at the University of Minnesota in 1991. The name Gopher comes from the university's mascot, the golden gopher. This GUI provides a hierarchical menu of directories and files. Users jump from general categories at high levels to more specific categories at lower levels until they find what they want. The information may reside on computers around the world.

Who Owns the Internet?

Although companies such as Netscape, Microsoft, MCI, IBM, and many others own pieces of Internet hardware and software, no single government, university or company owns or controls the entire Internet. Even at the hardware level—the fibers, wires, and routing equipment used to relay information—the Internet has no single owner. The main routers, which handle most of the traffic, are owned by several major data companies and organizations. Costs are shared among thousands of organizations, which pass costs on to the millions of users spread throughout the world. The Internet truly is a global infrastructure.

"It's in the nature of the Internet that distance is no object, and that resources are dispersed worldwide in hundreds or thousands of computers rather than held on massive central databases," says Joe Flower in *The Future of the Internet*. "Wonderfully cheap, efficient and interactive to use, a nightmare to cost."* In fact, the structure and methodology of the network make it almost impossible to charge people according to their activities on the Net or the strain they put on the network.

Over the years, governments have attempted to tax the Internet, prohibit certain kinds of activities from taking place over the Internet, monitor e-mails, and enact other regulations. All these attempts have failed. Remember the basic design goal: if one part of the network fails, communications are routed through another path. The Internet is decentralized; it is flexible; it is international. If the state of Kansas or the government of Canada decides to regulate Internet transactions, sites can easily move to computers in Florida or Denmark.

The closest thing the Internet has to a manager is a group of volunteers called the Internet Society (ISOC). Members are from around the world and all areas of interest, including government, telecommunications companies, public interest groups, and universities. It promotes cooperation and coordination for the Internet, but has no real power. "Nothing they do is enforceable. It's all enlightened self-interest," according to Vinton Cerf, founder of the ISOC. "The real secret behind the Internet is that it's a grass-roots, bottom-up system."**

* Joe Flower, "The Future of the Internet: An Overview," in *The Future of the Internet*, edited by Charles P. Cozic (San Diego, Calif.: Greenhaven Press, 1997), 14.

** Quoted in Flower, "The Future of the Internet," 12.

Before Gopher was developed, users had to log on to individual computers to search for information. Now a user could jump from a computer in Boston to one in Toyko, Mexico City, London, or Sydney without realizing it. Gopher users called this burrowing.

About the same time Gopher was being developed, software engineer Tim Berners-Lee was in Switzerland inventing the World Wide Web. Berners-Lee had been using the Internet for his work at CERN, the European Organization for Nuclear Research in Geneva, Switzerland. He thought that the user interface was ridiculous and wanted a system that was easy to use—a system in which you could point and click to access the documents you wanted to see. He wanted it badly enough to create it himself.

The original 20-page proposal for what came to be called the World Wide Web is still tacked to a wall in Berners-Lee's office. Amid a muddle of dashed lines, boxes, and arrows is the date March 1989. Berners-Lee says he encountered a lot of blank stares from his peers back then. Few people had the vision to see that this proposal would revolutionize communications.

Berners-Lee's system used the concept of hypertext, which allows links to be established between documents. Each document was encoded and displayed using HTML, HyperText Markup Language. Each document had its own address, later called a Uniform Resource Locator (URL). With a software program called a browser, users maneuvered through the documents, jumping from one to another without having to use cryptic commands or know the physical location of the document.

In *Weaving the Web,* Berners-Lee described his intentions:

When I proposed the Web in 1989, the driving force I had in mind was communication through shared knowledge, and the driving "market" for it was collaboration among people at work and at home. By building a hypertext Web, a group of people of whatever size could easily express themselves, quickly acquire and convey knowledge, overcome misunderstandings, and reduce duplication of effort. . . . The intention was that the Web be used as a personal information system, and a group tool on all scales, from the team of two creating a flyer for the local elementary school play to the world population deciding on ecological issues.[21]

At first, Berners-Lee had a difficult time getting people to see the potential of the Web. On September 13, 1991, he demonstrated the Web to American Paul Kunz, who was visiting the CERN laboratory. The system sparked Kunz's interest. When he went back home to the Stanford Linear Accelerator Center, Kunz designed a Web page containing about 200,000 references to scientific papers that he knew were of interest to physicists all over the world. On December 12, 1991, at 4:00 P.M., Kunz posted his page on Berners-Lee's Web; it was the first Web page on a U.S. computer.

In 1992, Berners-Lee gave away free to the public the World Wide Web software and its specifications. His tremendous generosity allowed everyone to use and create Web pages.

The Web quickly attracted users, including Marc Andreessen, a student at the University of Illinois at Champaign-Urbana and a part-time employee of the university's National Center for Supercomputing Applications (NCSA). Andreessen admired the Web but thought the text-based browser interface was too complicated.

In just three months, Andreessen and a friend created a browser that was easier to use, and it worked with graphics in addition to text. Remarkably, the program ended up having only 9,000 lines of code; Microsoft's Windows 95 had 11 million lines of code. Andreessen called the browser Mosaic and distributed it free on the Internet in early 1993.

Mosaic was an instant success. But Andreessen wasn't done yet. The first versions had been for use on UNIX computers, and by Thanksgiving, he released version for both the

IBM-compatible and Macintosh personal computers. Within a month, a million people were using Mosaic. Now users could transfer text and graphics. All they needed was a PC and Internet access. Suddenly, it was possible for millions of people to use the Internet from home. Andreessen was a hero.

A deep sense of community developed among Internet users. "New users were gently escorted around the Internet by veterans," explains author Douglas Rushkoff. "An experienced user delighted in setting up a newbie's connection. . . . To be an Internet user was to be an Internet advocate."[22]

Users quickly realized that cyberspace was not a prepackaged world; it was a place where they could design their own content. Programmers stayed up late creating new applications that would make the Internet a better place. Almost all software programs were distributed free of charge. "The Internet was built for love, not profit," says Rushkoff.[23]

Computer scientist Jaron Lanier wrote: "The Web was built by millions of people simply because they wanted it, without need, greed, fear, hierarchy, authority figures, ethnic identification, advertising, or any other form of manipulation. Nothing like this ever happened before in history. We can be blasé about it now, but it is what we will be remembered for. We have been made aware of a new dimension of human potential."[24]

The history of the Internet is largely filled with tales of collaboration; however, not every person or institution was without greed. At the NCSA, Andreessen's supervisors tried to split up the Mosaic programming team and take credit for inventing it. Andreessen was furious. He left Illinois for California's Silicon Valley and hooked up with millionaire Jim Clark, founder and former chairman of Silicon Graphics. Together they founded Mosaic Corporation with the intention of creating software called Mozilla, the Mosaic-Killer.

Andreessen and some of his old friends from NCSA teamed up to create a new and better browser. On October 11,

1994, the Navigator browser was available to download for free from the Internet. Within days, two million people were using Navigator. Seventy percent of Mosaic users switched to Navigator almost overnight.

It seemed that Andreessen had outwitted NCSA, but the battle wasn't over yet. NCSA sued him over the rights to the Navigator software and to the name Mosaic. As a result of the lawsuit, the company changed its name to Netscape Communications but retained the rights to its browser.

Andreessen had an even bigger battle waiting in the shadows. Bill Gates, chairman of Microsoft Corporation, was right on his heels. In 1995, Microsoft released its own Web browser, Internet Explorer. Then, on May 26, 1995, Bill Gates sent a memo to top Microsoft executives. Titled "The Internet Tidal Wave," it stated that he assigned to "the Internet the highest level of importance. In this memo I want to make clear that our focus on the Internet is critical to every part of our business." [25]

Gates was right, a tidal wave had hit. By the end of 1995, there were about 16 million users of computer communications networks. Gates realized that as people used their computers as network devices, the browser became the operating system. He knew he wanted a chunk of the browser market, so he started offering Internet Explorer for free. Within two years, Microsoft and Netscape had equal shares of the Web browser market.

The Web and its browsers revolutionized the Internet. They made the Internet accessible to the general public and of interest to businesses. Suddenly, the online world looked like a promising place for companies to advertise, promote, and sell products and services. By the year 2000, 56 percent of U.S. companies were selling their products online.

The Internet started with the cooperative efforts of government, industry, and academia. Now that small businesses and large corporations have entered the Internet arena, can cooperation continue? Science writer Barry Shell says: "The Internet, with its open, distributed structure, was designed to withstand a nuclear attack. If it can do that, it can withstand corporate America."[26]

3

The New Economy

AT ISSUE

"Until 1991, you had to sign an agreement promising not to conduct any business online just to get access to the Internet! Imagine that. It was a business-free zone," recalls journalist Douglas Rushkoff.[27] Of course, as soon as new legislation allowed commercial use of the Internet, businesses started marketing, advertising, and selling online. Financial investors provided piles of money to new Internet-based, dot-com companies. Before long, the Internet was boosting the New Economy of the 1990s.

Traditionally, investors expect a company to make a profit, but a new business model was at work. High sales volume, name recognition, and low losses were enough to boost a dot-com's stock, regardless of whether the company ever made a profit. Some financial analysts felt the dot-com stocks were greatly overvalued.

The party finally ended; over 500 Internet-based companies filed for bankruptcy or shut down in 2001. Was the Internet dead? Rushkoff said it was healthier than ever.

COMPANIES IN CYBERSPACE

A 1950 law stipulated that National Science Foundation computer networks could be used only for the job-related work of academics, scientists, and bureaucrats. Since the NSF managed the main Internet backbone, this statement meant that the Internet could not be used for commercial purposes. In 1991, an amendment to the law allowed use "for purposes in addition to research and education." The Internet was open for business.

Most pioneers from the ARPANET and the early years of the Internet resisted commercialization of the Internet. But Vint Cerf favored it, saying, "There had to be some business that made enough money to drive the network forward so I was very strongly in favour of commercialisation in order to get that economic engine turning."[28]

Radio stations were among the first of the traditional media to grasp the potential of the Internet. A website could provide listeners with information and program schedules. It could also offer pictures and graphics in conjunction with a broadcast. Discussion forums and e-mail exchanges came into use, too. Eventually, many radio stations were broadcasting online. Their audience was no longer the college campus or the county, it was the world.

In April 1994, the Internet Shopping Network (ISN) went online. Brick-and-mortar malls and stores put up Web pages to promote sales and special events. Mail order catalogs offered the option of ordering online. Department stores and drugstores started offering products online, too.

The commercialization of the Internet helped spur economic growth in the United States from 1995 to 1998. It helped create what was called the New Economy. The Encyclopedia of the New Economy, prepared by Wired Digital, Inc., explains, "When we talk about the new economy, we're talking about a world in which people work with their brains instead of their hands. A world in which communications technology creates global competition—not just for running shoes and laptop computers, but also for bank loans and other services that can't be packed into a crate and shipped."[29]

The old economy was about large companies facing limited competition in stable markets, mostly manufacturing goods. The New Economy was all about fast-growing, entrepreneurial companies in very competitive markets. The

One of the tools with which the World Wide Web has revolutionized society is online shopping. Consumers no longer have to leave their homes to purchase items that range from the mundane, such as drug items and cleaning supplies, to books, clothing, and original artwork. All of these items and more can be purchased online using a credit card or a customer's banking information.

ability to innovate and get to market fast was becoming an important competitive advantage.

Software entrepreneur Jim Bidzos observed:

> We saw the arrival of Internet time, which some people equate with dog years. It's seven times faster. But in Internet time there are no secrets. There is no time for delay. There are plenty of competitors who are going to eat you alive. Basically, what you need to do is get from the beginning to the end of a process, a mission, a sales effort, a product development cycle, you need to not take a breath, and start over and do it again as soon as you get done with one.... That's how you compete and survive if you're in the software business on the Internet.[30]

The result was new business rules, new sorts of organizations, and globalization. Location, a physical atmosphere, and in-person customer service were absent in these virtual stores. Online retailers eliminated the high costs of storefront rental, maintenance, and sales clerks. They might also have a small inventory. The theory was that an online store could operate more cheaply, and thus sell more cheaply. In many cases, products were sold at prices so far below those in traditional storefronts that they were often sold at a loss.

In some cases, online stores gave products away. Blue Mountain Arts Publishing, started by two former hippies, provided free online greeting cards, complete with images and music, to billions of users. Before long, Bluemountain.com was getting a million hits a day. And people were not only sending cards, they were ordering flowers, candy, and gifts. The Excite@Home website bought the card company for about $1 billion.

One of the most famous sites that gave things away was Napster, run by a red-haired 18-year-old. His website became the world's biggest online free-music system. Napster allowed millions of people to swap musical recordings every day. The record business was furious and filed suit against the Napster site. The settlement forced Napster to charge a monthly fee to its users and split the money between those creating, producing, and delivering the music.

The new business philosophy and "time-warping mentality" of Internet companies is explained by technology analyst J. Neil Weintraut:

> Tossing aside just about every business experience-honed tenet of business to build businesses in a methodical fashion, Internet businesses have adopted a grow-at-any-cost, without-any-revenue, claim-as-much-market-real-estate-before-anyone-moves-in approach to business. This mentality has come to be known as "Get Big Fast." . . . This is the hyper-growth, hyper-speed, hyper-bucks business world of the Internet.[31]

Get Big Fast meant offering low prices in the hope of building a large customer base and creating customer loyalty. Satisfied users would tell other users, who would spread the word. Then, in the future, the company could boost prices and profits would come. Many experts worried that such low prices may not be sustainable. In many cases, the experts were right; companies simply ran out of money to give away.

It also turned out that marketing these sites was expensive. The programmers who maintained these sites were also expensive, many of them earning four times the salary of a sales clerk. Doing business on the Internet was not as cheap as it had once seemed.

Many websites turned to advertising as a source of income. Ad banners ran across the top of Web pages and urged the visitor to "Click Here!" These banners did create brand-name awareness and lead to sales, but retailers wanted more than this random approach. They wanted to target ads to the potential interests of the user. Sites began to monitor the behavior of visitors to determine what ads to post.

For example, if a visitor typed "beagle" in a search screen, the site might respond by placing a banner ad for dog food on the next page. If a visitor entered a zip code to request a weather report for Denver, the site might respond with a banner ad for a theater in that city.

More recently, banner ads have been replaced by pop-up ads. When a user visits a website, the Web page loads and then other windows open to display some kind of advertisement. Most users find pop-up ads annoying, and online services have started bowing to their customers' complaints. AOL, MSN, and iVillage have vowed to eliminate most pop-up ads.

To earn money, some online retailers gathered intimate details about their customers and offered to sell information to marketers.

Some sites gather information about visitors by using a tool called a cookie. When a user visits a site, it places a cookie, a tiny tag of data, on his hard disk. The cookie can identify his browser (in essence, the user) as a unique entity. Every time the user returns to that site, the cookie can be retrieved and his behavior within the site can be tracked. In this way, advertisements might be customized to fit the user's interests, which are determined by what he accessed on the website. Or, the information gathered might be sold to marketers.

"Whether you sell stock or sell suits, the Internet has changed the world," says New York Stock Exchange chairman Richard A. Grasso.[32] In the financial world, investors traditionally consulted brokers when buying and selling stocks. Now, millions of new investors are trading stocks online, bypassing the brokers and their high fees. Websites provide instant access to stock prices, financial research, up-to-the-minute business news, and graphs of stock performance. The investor can decide what stock to purchase and pay a very small commission.

By the end of 1999, an estimated 10 million investors were trading online. Trading on the Internet accounts for 25 percent of all retail securities investing. Much of this activity is generated by day traders, people who exclusively trade stocks online, usually from their home.

"The effect on the market, experts agree, has been major," wrote author Robert Shapiro in 1999. "Many observers see the actions of day traders as a key factor, perhaps *the* key factor, that has driven Internet stocks sky high. It's how a company like Amazon.com . . . which isn't expected to make a profit until 2003, increased in value tenfold in 1998."[33]

Day trading demonstrates how the Internet is eliminating middlemen. It allows people to bypass stockbrokers, retailers, distributors, editors, professors, and other intermediaries. Perhaps the best example is the online auction house eBay. The only middleman between individual buyers and sellers is eBay itself; all other layers have been stripped away.

Sellers on eBay do not need a storefront, contacts among collectors, or knowledge of collectibles and their worth. They get access to millions of potential buyers by using eBay, and the marketplace sets the price.

These employees at Amazon.com on December 15, 1999, were busy heeding the company founder's motto: Work Hard, Have Fun, and Make History. Jeff Bezos, who started Amazon.com in 1995, has consistently emphasized good customer service and, in the process, built sales up to billions of dollars annually and provided a model for successful e-commerce.

Many companies fear that online business will replace the traditional business environment. So far, however, that logic has not always been sound. In the financial market, the influx of online stock trading has meant more, not less, business for Wall Street. And Amazon.com has proven that the same is true for the book market.

Amazon did not take sales away from traditional retailers, it enhanced book sales. Big chain stores make money selling books on the best-sellers list, while Amazon is successful with other titles. "What the publishers get excited about," said Amazon vice president David Risher, "is that we can revitalize a midlist or

Amazon.com

Amazon.com is perhaps one of the most ironic Internet-based companies. Millions of people use the hot technological invention—the Internet, which is supposed to provide everything you need online—to buy old-fashioned, printed-on-paper books. Who could have predicted the swift adoption of a new means of commerce, and yet the steadfastness of traditional media such as books?

The company's motto, "Work Hard, Have Fun, and Make History,"* is often repeated by founder Jeff Bezos. In 1995, Bezos quit his high-paying job in New York City, moved to Seattle, and started Amazon.com in the garage of his rented house. He picked the name Amazon because it started with the letter A, securing it an early position in phone book and other business listings, and because it is recognized around the world as Earth's biggest river.

Amazon.com was built on low overhead of operations, fast turnover of inventory, and an obsession with customer service. Bezos realized that one happy customer will do more than tell five friends; he will use e-mail, newsgroups, and listservs to tell 5,000 people.

Although Amazon.com started by selling printed books, it always strived to "Get Big Fast," and now it defines itself as a site where customers can find anything they might want to buy online. As the company grew, it kept losing money, but its stock went through the roof. What impressed onlookers in 1998 and 1999 were the billions of dollars in sales. Even "brick-and-mortar" companies like General Motors looked at Amazon.com as a model for e-commerce. *Time* magazine chose Bezos as its Person of the Year in 1999.

However, in early 2001, Amazon laid off 1,300 employees, about 15 percent of its workforce, and closed one of its distribution sites. Despite the bad times, in his book about Amazon.com, Robert Spector was still upbeat: "One thing is certain: even if Amazon.com went out of business tomorrow, it will have made an enormous impact on how business has changed at the end of the twentieth century and the beginning of the twenty-first. Virtually every company, regardless of size, has changed its thinking because of Amazon.com."**

* Robert Spector, *Amazon.com: Get Big Fast* (New York: HarperBusiness, 2000), 223.

** Spector, *Amazon.com,* 233..

even backlist book by featuring it or by helping them target a book to a specialized audience." [34]

An estimated $3 billion changed hands online during the 1998 holiday season. In 1999, 17 million U.S. households shopped online and online sales topped $20 billion. While those sales amounted to less than .5 percent of U.S. consumer spending, they spurred economic growth. From 1993 to 1998, the information technology sectors were growing at double the rate of the overall U.S. economy. For example, the Internet created 1.1 million new jobs in 1996.

In 2001, *Fortune* magazine asked General Electric's legendary CEO Jack Welch, "Where do you think we are as an economy as far as e-business goes?" Welch quickly replied, "First inning." [35]

THE RISE AND FALL OF THE DOT-COM EMPIRE

In June 1999, *Business Week* reported, "In industry after industry, Corporate America is suddenly feeling the uncomfortable gnaw of Internet Anxiety—a stomach-churning mixture of envy, resentment, and increasingly, just plain fear. . . . After all, with the Goldman Sachs Internet Index (GIN) climbing a phenomenal 453% between last September and its early April high, who wouldn't get a little green watching from the sidelines? . . . The lucky devils running Net businesses are getting filthy rich besides." [36]

Netscape was one of the first companies to show it was possible to strike it rich with an Internet business. In 1995, in an initial public offering, shares of its stock had been priced at $28, but opened at $70. A new business model had developed.

Investors began to supply cash for many Internet-based companies. "The Internet was merely the sexy word, the come-hither, the bright idea at the top of the pyramid," observed journalist Douglas Rushkoff.[37]

The excitement surrounding Internet start-ups reached President Clinton, who in 1997 noted, "It will literally be possible to start a company tomorrow, and next week do business in

Japan and Germany and Chile, all without leaving your home, something that used to take years and years and years to do."[38]

The notion was wondrous, yet it was not yet clear how an online company like Yahoo! could give things away and still make money. The free site was founded by David Filo and Jerry Yang, two graduate students at Stanford. They started exchanging the addresses of their favorite sites and devised a system of categories to index them. Then they selected a cool name, Yahoo!, for their website and it became an overnight success.

YAHOO!

In February 1994, David Filo and Jerry Yang were graduate students working out of a trailer at Stanford University. As a hobby, they started keeping lists of their favorite websites. The lists soon became so big that they had to create categories and subcategories. Before long, they developed a website called Jerry and David's Guide to the World Wide Web. That name seemed too boring, so they looked through the dictionary for a better name.

They chose Yahoo!, an acronym for Yet Another Hierarchical Officious Oracle. Filo and Yang insist that the true reason they selected the name was the definition of a yahoo: "rude, unsophisticated, uncouth."*

Yahoo! was the first online navigational guide to the Web, and hundreds of people started using it. Word spread, and by the fall of 1994, Yahoo! was celebrating its first day of a million hits, which translated into 100,000 unique visitors. Filo and Yang knew they had stumbled onto something big.

In March 1995, the two students incorporated the business and started talking with venture capitalists. In May 1996, Yahoo's first TV commercial aired. It introduced the famous line: "Do You Yahoo!?"

Yahoo! now describes itself as "a leading global Internet communications, commerce and media company that offers a comprehensive branded network of services to more than 237 million individuals each month worldwide."**

* Yahoo! Media Relations, "The History of Yahoo! How It All Started. . . ."
<http://docs.yahoo.com/info/misc/history.html>

** Yahoo!, "History of Yahoo!"

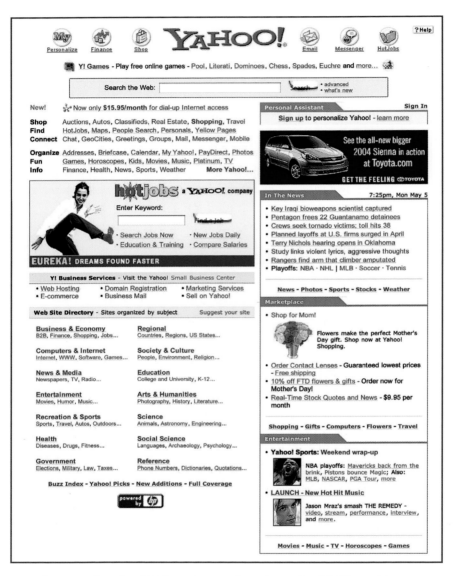

In early 1994, Stanford University grad students David Filo and Jerry Yang started what became Yahoo! by posting lists of their favorite websites on their own website. By that fall, the first online navigational guide to the Web was getting a million hits a day and on its way to becoming a household word.

Even though Yahoo!'s services are free, the site interested investors because it had so many visitors. Filo and Yang's plan was that Yahoo! would make money by selling advertisements. That was the business strategy for many Internet-based companies.

Many success stories were exaggerated or distorted. According to venture capitalist Art Berliner, "A lot of this was driven because they were giving stuff away. That was a great deal for the consumer. It was not so great for the companies."[39]

In the middle of 2000, the bottom dropped out of the Internet economy. By October 2000, handfuls of Internet companies were declaring bankruptcy or shutting down completely. Among the casualties was Chipshot.com, a site that sold golf equipment. The company had raised $50 million, and spent it all.

According to Webmergers.com, a San Francisco research firm, 225 dot-com companies failed in 2000. At least 537 failed in 2001. During the first six months of 2002, 93 or more Internet companies failed. The dot-coms became "dot-toast." Businesses such as Garden.com, Living.com, Toysmart.com, Eve.com, Craftshop.com, BBQ.com, and Babygear.com were all gone.

"To those of us who really love it, the Internet is looking and feeling more social, more alive, more participatory, and more, well, more Internet-y than ever before," wrote Douglas Rushkoff in *Yahoo! Internet Life* in July 2001.[40] Rushkoff backed up his assertion with statistics that showed Internet use had increased despite the dot-com bust. "We spent an average of 20.2 hours looking at Internet sites in March 2001, up from 15.9 hours last year and 12.8 hours the year before," he wrote. Even more surprising was the fact that although many dot-coms had failed, e-commerce had risen more than 30 percent compared with the previous year.

Jim Romeo, author of *Net Know-How: Surviving the Bloodbath,* advises Internet companies to go back to the basics. He says, "You need to follow the same principles that created the industrial revolution and built the wealth of nations."[41] He tells dot-com companies to strive for profit, not just market share, and to minimize expenses and not expand too quickly. Romeo says they need to be realistic about funding, too. The word "Internet" in a business plan no longer makes investors swarm to your door.

Even the favored Internet companies were having a tough time financially. Internet stocks had lost much of their value, and investors were struggling to figure out the companies' real value. One result of businesses trying to impress investors by showing profits was that websites that had always provided free access to their content started to charge fees.

News provider CNN now charges users to view video clips on its website. Some newspapers charge to access their online versions. Others, such as *The New York Times* and *Christian Science Monitor*, charge for access to archived stories.

Even Yahoo! is now under pressure to make money. The company reported a loss of $53.6 million for the first quarter of 2002, up from a $11.5 million loss for the same period in the previous year. Like many other websites, Yahoo! is increasing fees for its premium services, such as forwarding mail to other accounts. That does not mean that users will flee, according to Debashis Aikat, a University of North Carolina professor who specializes in Internet culture. "I can bet you that even if fees doubled, there will be a backlash," he says, "but the people who need it will use it, and that's what [the Internet companies] want. They're trying to find really good customers." [42]

In today's business environment, really good customers means paying customers. Internet companies need to make a profit. Though the New Economy was often said to have changed everything, it did not change the need for companies to make money. "I think the business model is shifting and becoming more realistic," Aikat says.

That does not mean that the New Economy was a myth. According to the 2002 New Economy Index, produced by the Progressive Policy Institute in Washington, D.C., the recent economic downturn is a "bump along the way" in the reshaping of the economy and society. The report further states:

> In all regards, it looks like the worst is behind us and we are poised for a period of robust New Economy growth, perhaps less spectacular than the dizzying days of 2000, but strong all the same. It's clear that this was more than a one-time burst of energy that has dissipated. Rather, we've barely scratched the surface of New Economy digital transformation. To paraphrase Mark Twain, reports of the New Economy's demise have been greatly exaggerated.[43]

THE NEWFANGLED WORKPLACE

Besides the changes in commerce and business models, the Internet brought changes to the workplace, changes that went beyond using e-mail for communications and an intranet for computer operations. Companies have become global and so has the workplace. Businesses and employees are now free of geographic constraints, some so much so that they occupy only virtual space.

According to a Deloitte & Touche report, telecommuting accounted for 45 percent of all new jobs from 1987 to 1992. Electronic communication enables more than 80 percent of full-time American employees to work either off-site or with those who are off-site.

"It's a challenge to our mental model," says Arlene Johnson of WFD Consulting, which conducted a study of telecommuters. "So many things assume a central workplace, with those who work elsewhere out of the norm, the exception, the oddity. In fact, working over a distance seems to be the new norm. The future is now—it's already a reality."[44]

Companies that allow employees to telecommute reap real advantages in employee productivity, retention, and commitment. Telecommuters tend to work longer hours, but are less likely to feel physically and emotionally drained at the end of the day. However, some workers do report feeling lonely and isolated from the work group.

A recent study of the U.S. economy describes a "free-agent nation" composed of 25 million workers who are self-employed or independent contractors. In large part, new technologies such as the Internet have created this fast-growing sector because they allow these "lone eagles" to work from almost anywhere they want.

Lee Taylor managed several technical writers for a California firm before he moved to Telluride, Colorado, to become a lone eagle. Taylor now works as a freelance consultant. He took a large pay cut, but his housing costs are lower and he can enjoy midweek skiing.

Noorin Khwaya is a traditional Muslim woman who stays home to care for her children near Daytona Beach, Florida. But she is also the CEO of TwoMuslimGirls.com. Through her website, Khwaya sells head scarves, long overgarments, and Islamic wedding dresses, which she and a friend design and manufacture. In the first two months of operation, her site had a 500 percent rise in demand. Customers are from Idaho, North Dakota, and other states across the country.

The global reach of the Internet enables consultants and employees to reside anywhere in the world. Workers in less developed countries can work for American companies without having to relocate. The "international split shift" is a reality. A day shift of U.S. workers can complete certain tasks for another shift of workers overseas to finish and transmit the results back to the U.S. workers in time for their arrival in the morning. It has even been suggested that workers in Africa could monitor closed-circuit security systems in American shopping malls.

In addition to creating a global workplace, the Internet has launched many mergers and acquisitions. AOL bought Netscape, and later the large cable network Time Warner. Deutsche Telekom, France Telecom, and Sprint formed an alliance called Global One to provide worldwide voice, data, and video service. Microsoft partnered with NBC to create the MSNBC network, which uses its television network to introduce people to the online world and makes its online service a part of the way people use TV.

How is this newfangled workplace affecting the workers who create all those Web pages, write all that online content, monitor those chat rooms, work the help desks, and design new technology? In *NetSlaves,* Bill Lessard and Steve Baldwin offer accounts of long hours, countless meals of pizza and soda, poor management, and chronic backstabbing. Working in the Internet business means "the complete absence of a social life, a lousy diet, lack of exercise, chain smoking, repetitive stress disorders, and last but not least, hemorrhoids."[45]

Challenges for Law and Government

"There is material on the Internet that is clearly inappropriate for children," stated President Clinton in 1996. "As a parent, I understand the concerns that parents have about their children accessing inappropriate material. . . . We can and must develop a solution for the Internet . . . that protects children in ways that are consistent with America's free speech values."[46] Developing solutions to the committing of objectionable acts and outright crime on the Internet is not easy. Would increased regulation limit free speech and dampen the creative and entrepreneurial growth of the Internet?

INTERNET CRIME

The U.S. government contributed money and incentive to the development of the Internet. Eventually, the network was turned over to research institutions and then to commercial businesses. The government said farewell to their control over the Internet. But it wasn't that simple. This new communication medium became a target of criminals and mischief-makers, and the government has taken on the roles of guard and cop.

Some new kinds of crime sprang up on the Internet, but most often, new twists were added to old schemes. Software piracy—the unauthorized duplication of copyrighted software— had been an issue since the first PCs were sold. But the Internet changed the situation by hosting online copies that can be distributed quickly and repeatedly. In 1998, the Software

Along with the advantages of the Internet has come crime, including attacks by hackers on e-commerce sites. In February 2000, President Bill Clinton met with industry professionals and academics to discuss a new Internet security plan developed in response to several such attacks.

Publishers Association charged that more than $11 billion per year was lost due to illegal duplication of computer programs.

Worms were another problem. A worm is a self-replicating, self-propagating program; it runs and multiplies itself without assistance from users. The first computer worms were actually designed to do work, like post announcements throughout networks. Soon, however, worms were doing other tasks.

On November 2, 1988, a Cornell University graduate student, Robert Morris Jr. uploaded a worm program to the Internet. He soon discovered that the program was replicating itself and infecting machines at a much faster rate than he had anticipated. Morris tried to send a message telling programmers how to kill the worm but it was too late—the network was already clogged. The worm temporarily disabled 6,000 of the 60,000 host computers at universities, military sites, and medical research facilities, costing each site from $200 to more than $53,000 to fix.

After a few days, Morris was named as the author of the worm. He was convicted of violating the Computer Fraud and Abuse Act (Title 18) and sentenced to three years of probation, 400 hours of community service, and a fine of $10,050 and the costs of his supervision.

By the late 1980s, computer enthusiasts were gaining access to computer systems in corporations and other organizations. These hackers were proficient at writing software programs, debugging systems, and identifying vulnerabilities and weaknesses in computer systems and networks. Most broke into systems out of curiosity and to prove that they could find holes in security systems; they stole nothing and destroyed nothing. But some did change records or commit credit card fraud.

In the first half of 1990, Secret Service agents began a nationwide crackdown on computer hackers. The effort, code-named Operation SunDevil, included 27 searches of suspected hackers' homes and offices. Authorities seized 40 computer systems, over 20,000 disks, and lots of other equipment. They arrested several young people.

Some people were concerned that the constitutional rights of Internet users were being taken rather lightly. They formed a civil liberties group called the Electronic Frontier Foundation (EFF). The group's mission is "to help civilize the electronic frontier; to make it truly useful and beneficial not just to a technical elite, but to everyone; and to do this in a way which is in keeping with our society's highest traditions of the free and open flow of information and communication." [47]

The EFF was founded by John Barlow, a writer, politician, and former lyricist for the Grateful Dead; John Gilmore of Sun Microsystems, and Mitchell Kapor, founder of Lotus 1-2-3. It

The Steve Jackson Case

Steve Jackson was the owner of a computer-game company that was raided in 1990 as part of the government's crackdown on hackers, code-named Operation SunDevil. U.S. Secret Service agents were tracking the distribution of a document that had been illegally copied from a Bell-South computer. The document described how the emergency 911 system worked. One of the alleged recipients of the document was an employee of Steve Jackson.

The Secret Service took all of Jackson's computers and data, and even copies of an upcoming game book. Jackson's business was nearly ruined and he was forced to lay off almost half of his employees. Eventually, the Secret Service returned all of the computers and did not press charges against the company, because they were unable to find a copy of the 911 system document on the computers.

When Jackson inspected the returned computers, he was furious. All of the e-mail that had been stored on the company's electronic bulletin board had been read and erased. Jackson believed his rights as a publisher and the free speech and privacy rights of his users had been violated. He found other techies who agreed that civil liberties issues were involved.

Mitch Kapor, former president of Lotus Development Corporation, John Perry Barlow, former lyricist for the Grateful Dead, and John Gilmore of Sun Microsystems formed the Electronic Frontier Foundation (EFF) to work on civil liberties issues raised by new technologies. They represented Steve Jackson Games in a lawsuit brought against the Secret Service. The judge awarded Jackson $50,000 in lost profits and deemed the seizure of his equipment unlawful.

"The Steve Jackson Games case turned out to be an extremely important one in the development of a proper legal framework for cyberspace," states the EFF website. "For the first time, a court held that electronic mail deserves at least as much protection as telephone calls. We take for granted today that law enforcement must have a warrant that particularly describes all electronic mail messages before seizing and reading them. The Steve Jackson Games case established that principle."*

* Electronic Frontier Foundation,"About EFF." <http://www.eff.org/abouteff.html>

surprised many people that Kapor, a respected corporate executive, would put up $200,000 to fund what seemed like a radical hacker organization. Kapor explained, "There was uninformed and panicky government response, treating situations like they were threats to national security. They were in the process of trying to put some of these kids away for a long time and throw away the key, and it just felt like there were injustices being done out of sheer lack of understanding. I felt a moral outrage. Barlow and I felt something had to be done."[48]

Secret Service assistant special agent Dale Boll defended the government probe. "We have not declared war," he said. "Computer crime is a serious offense, but we don't overreact."[49] The authors of *The History of the Internet* noted the significance of this event: "The 'hackdown' and the birth of the EFF signaled a fundamental change in the federal government's relationship to its baby, the Net. The government goes from being the Internet's proud parent—its funder, nurturer, and cheerleader— to its disciplinarian and cop."[50]

One of the most notorious hackers was Kevin Mitnick. The hacker community portrayed him as a curious young man who was a scapegoat for law enforcement and an example of the government's suppression of civil rights. The media depicted Mitnick as a criminal because in 1989, he had served a year in jail for computer fraud. Not long after his release, police saw signs of illegal behavior and sought to arrest him again in 1992.

Mitnick eluded the police. Over the next three years, he allegedly tried to obtain a false driver's license, removed files from a research computer, and stole thousands of credit card numbers. One of his techniques was to simply call a corporation, pretend to be from the computer department, and ask for the network password. Eventually Mitnick was caught and jailed; he was denied bail and use of a computer. To protest this treatment, hackers replaced the regular screens at the websites of Yahoo!, UNICEF, and *The New York Times* with screens calling for

Convicted hacker Kevin Mitnick served four years in federal prison for stealing computer secrets from companies. Here he is seen with his attorney in June 2000, protesting his probation officer's refusal to allow him to become a columnist for an Internet company.

support for Mitnick. After serving his time, Mitnick was released in January 2000.

There are plenty of other cases of mischief and crime. In February 1996, a hacker broke into a network at the Los Alamos

National Laboratory, the government lab that developed the atomic bomb. In 1989, a German spy hacked into U.S. military systems and sold the information to Soviet intelligence officers. His scheme was thwarted by an alert systems manager, Cliff Stoll, who recounted the events in *The Cuckoo's Egg.* In February 2000, hackers bombarded the E*Trade brokerage website with data. They overloaded the E*Trade system and prevented thousands of users from accessing the site and trading stocks.

The Internet has reached all corners of society, good and bad, and all corners of the globe. In 1996, Central Intelligence Agency Director John Deutch expressed his concern that the United States is more vulnerable to information warfare tactics due to businesses' reliance on telecommunications and networks. "Virtually any single 'bad actor' can acquire the hardware and software needed to attack some of our critical information-based infrastructures," he said. "We have evidence that a number of countries around the world are developing the doctrine, strategies and tools to conduct information attacks."[51]

Because the Internet is a borderless place, it is difficult to determine whose laws apply in cases involving its use. Laws about consumer protection, privacy, intellectual property, banking, securities, taxes, and gaming vary from nation to nation. And those laws keep changing as government authorities try to write and approve laws quickly enough to keep up with the rapidly changing technology.

CENSORSHIP, COOKIES, AND OTHER CONCERNS

By 1993, U.S. law enforcement was dealing with a new problem: the online pornographer. Antiporn groups pushed for government regulations against online smut. Civil liberty groups said the prevalence of online porn was overblown. In 1995, the debate broke wide open.

The cover article of the July 3 issue of *Time* magazine was entitled: "On a Screen Near You: Cyberporn." Journalist Philip Elmer-DeWitt claimed that pornography was easily available to children on the Internet and cited a study done by Marty Rimm at Carnegie Mellon University as proof. Rimm suggested that 83.5 percent of Internet graphics were pornographic.

Panic ensued before the truth was revealed: Rimm's research was flawed. Rimm had evaluated adult-oriented bulletin board systems that were not connected to the Internet and that generally required a credit card. The true estimate of pornographic images on the Internet was less than 1 percent.

A flurry of e-mails, newsgroup mailings, and other postings harshly criticized Elmer-DeWitt for writing the story. He eventually admitted that he had "screwed up" and *Time* recanted the story. Clearly, the Internet was a forum that allowed users to challenge the power of the established Big Media.

Meanwhile, the story had already stirred action; the U.S. Senate had proposed a bill to deal with the alleged reams of Internet porn. As a result, on February 6, 1996, President Clinton signed the Communications Decency Act (CDA), which made it illegal to use the Internet to distribute to people under eighteen years of age any message "that, in context, depicts or describes, in terms patently offensive as measured by contemporary standards, sexual or excretory activities or organs." Offenses were punishable by $100,000 fines and imprisonment.

The CDA immediately received criticism from the EFF, the American Civil Liberties Union (ACLU), and other organizations. Lisa Kamm of the ACLU said, "things which would be protected, were they published in a newspaper, or said over the telephone, were suddenly illegal acts under [the CDA], simply because they occurred over the Internet."[52] The groups filed a lawsuit challenging the act.

The Justice Department did not enforce the CDA while the case was in progress. Ultimately, the U.S. Supreme Court found the decency provision unconstitutional. The decision was that "the interest in encouraging freedom of expression in a democratic society outweighs any theoretical but unproven benefit of censorship."

The court's decision took away from the government the responsibility for control content and access and gave it back to parents and individuals. Schools and parents began to use filters or blocking software to limit children's access to websites with pornography and hate speech. Some people formed regulating groups like CyberAngels to try to make the Web a safer place. They patrol the Internet looking for evidence of child pornography, sexual predators, and other online criminal content, which they then report to law enforcement.

However, citizen regulation and blocking software do not work perfectly, either. The software must be updated regularly to keep up with new sites, and enterprising children can bypass software filters.

Pressure on the government to enact controls continued, so they passed the Children's Online Privacy Protection Act (COPPA) in 1998. It required websites that collect personal information from children under age 13 to comply with several rules. These sites have to post their privacy policy, get parental consent for a child's access, and allow parents to review all personal information collected from their child.

Not everyone agrees with the policies of COPPA, and the issue is still being debated. "The Internet is largely an unregulated environment and, no matter how many net experts tell us it's a safe place to hang out, we all know that it can be a haven for pedophiles and racists," writes journalist Gail Robinson. "There's a battle going on between old-school net purists, who think that any form of government regulation is heavy-handed censorship, and the new breed of net users, who want to protect their families from the seamier side of the net. We have to recognise that, now the net has forced its way into our homes, the content has to be regulated, just like the programmes we see on television."[53]

Pornographic material is a huge concern, and so is the growing prevalence of hate speech on the Internet. Regulation is virtually impossible because of the international nature of the Internet and the differing laws regarding hate speech. In

Germany, it is illegal to promote Nazi ideology. In many European countries, it is illegal to deny the reality of the Holocaust. In the United States, the First Amendment to the Constitution guarantees freedom of speech, even to those whose opinions are objectionable to the mainstream public.

As with porn, using filtering software is one option for avoiding hate speech. The Anti-Defamation League (ADL) developed a software filter called the HateFilter that blocks access to certain sites. The blocked sites include those that advocate bigotry, hatred, or violence towards Jews or other groups on the basis of religion, race, ethnicity, or sexual orientation. The use of such filters at public institutions, such as schools and libraries, has been debated since it limits the rights of access. A compromise is to allow unrestricted use for adults, but to provide supervised (filtered) access for children.

The U.S. Constitution guarantees every citizen the right to privacy, but some observers feel that the Internet threatens that right. According to a 1998 study, 92 percent of websites collect personal information from online consumers. Many Web servers track where users click during a visit and what site the user came from. When users fill out forms to enter contests, order products, or take surveys, they leave more information. The use of this information is what concerns people. Some sites sell it to other companies. America Online did; they let telemarketers use members' phone numbers. After receiving complaints from outraged clients, AOL reversed its policy.

Privacy advocates have complained about the practices at Yahoo!, where members who want to tell the company not to share their e-mail addresses and interests or send unwanted e-mail offers have to click through more than a dozen boxes to make their choices known. And even after this time-consuming process, the company reserves the right to "update this policy," possibly voiding the members' stated preferences.

Many sites place tiny files called cookies on the hard drive of a visitor's computer. The cookie tracks the visitor's movements throughout the site and might collect information about purchases. Data gathered by the cookie can then be matched with any user-supplied information and a personal profile starts to emerge. In many cases, cookies are useful. They may store passwords and user IDs so a user does not have to keep retyping them every time they visit. Information from the cookie might also be used to make "Personal Recommendations" or to display information for the visitor.

Some users consider cookies objectionable because the information might be sold to junk mailers or telemarketers. A feature in most browsers allows users to disallow cookies or to notify the user before a cookie is created. However, cookies are so prevalent that if you choose the latter option, you will probably be swamped with pop-up windows.

"I think cookies could be the death of the Internet," says one marketing executive. "I think they're insidious. I realize the need for good, solid tracking information, and I have no problem with that. The problem is that they're hidden, and that's an invasion of electronic privacy." [54]

People do not want their e-mail In Box filled with unsolicited mass e-mails, known as "spam." They are mostly just a nuisance for users, but they clog network transmissions and burden the computers of Internet service providers. If users inform their ISP about spam, the ISP can then take action against the spammer.

It is not just ads that are a problem. Because e-mail can be mass distributed with one click of a mouse, numerous hoaxes and scams propagate on the Internet. One hoax promised to pay $1,000 to anyone who forwarded a copy of the phony e-mail. The message claimed that Bill Gates was testing a new e-mail tracking program and would send a $1,000 check to those who participated. No one ever received a check.

On Thursday, July 31, 1997, an e-mail message circulated with the text of a commencement speech supposedly given by author Kurt Vonnegut at MIT. It was witty and whimsical, starting with "Ladies and gentlemen of the class of '97, wear sunscreen." But the author of the imaginary speech was not Vonnegut, it was newspaper columnist Mary Schmich. It is still unknown who originated the hoax.

People's great concern about computer viruses made them vulnerable to a hoax about a virus. An e-mail with the subject "good times" warned about the "good times" virus and other viruses. In fact, the so-called virus was harmless, but the message circulated repeatedly.

E-mail also created a new means of spreading real computer viruses. One of the most notorious e-mail viruses was 1999's Melissa virus. An unsuspecting user received an e-mail message from a friend that read, "Here is that document you asked for . . . don't show it to anyone else ;-)." The attached Word document contained a list of passwords for pornographic sites, but it also contained a virus. Once the attached document was opened, the virus sent a copy of the message and the attachment to the first 50 names in the address book. Within minutes, 50 more people received messages that infected their computers.

The Melissa virus did not actually harm users' computers, but some e-mail servers crashed due to the swarm of messages. Viruses such as this cost millions of dollars in lost productivity and created a market for antivirus programs. These software programs continuously monitor the system, looking for suspicious activity. Since new viruses are always being created, antivirus programs must be updated on a regular basis.

The advent of the Internet required reworking the copyright laws. Copyright is basically the legal exclusive right of the author of a creative work to control the copying of that work. For works transmitted online, authors may copyright works consisting of text, artwork, music, audiovisual material (including any sounds), sound recordings, and so on. But it can be difficult to prevent the copying of copyrighted works.

"The Internet is one gigantic copying machine," says David Nimmer, a Los Angeles lawyer. "All copyrighted works can now

In April 1999, David L. Smith pleaded guilty to a charge of knowingly spreading a computer virus with the intent to cause damage. Smith's Melissa virus caused more than $80 million in damages, infected more than a million PCs in North America, and disrupted business and government computer networks.

be digitised, and once on the Net, copying is effortless, costless, widespread, and immediate."[55]

Part of the solution is to educate people about copyright laws. For example, works are copyrighted the moment they are written, and no copyright notice is required. Copyright is violated whether the person who made the illegal copy was paid money for the copy or gave it away for free. Postings to the Internet are not part of the public domain, and permission to do further copying must be obtained. Publicly posting a private e-mail is technically a violation, but simply revealing facts from an e-mail is not. The law is not really intended to protect works with no commercial value.

Another new issue involves trademarks and domain names. In cyberspace, a company's identity is established by its domain name, such as www.disney.com. Companies have to register their trademark names in cyberspace or risk losing their trademark to someone else.

Some savvy Internet users started cyber-squatting—registering potentially valuable domain names and hoping to sell the name to a company for a big payout. Reportedly, Microsoft paid $10,000 for www.slate.com, the website of a Microsoft-funded online magazine. Other companies have sued to get their trademark name as their domain name. Volkswagen won a case against VirtualWorks to get the VW.net name.

Internet regulations and laws continue to be written and rewritten as the technology develops. And because the Internet is a forum, issues are certain to be exposed and widely debated.

5

Changing Social Modes

AT ISSUE

The Internet allows us to connect with the entire world. Some analysts say it brings people together and offers unbounded sociability. Some feel it alienates users from family and friends. Others wonder about the social value of online communities in which members can be anonymous.

What about those who are not connected to the Internet? The Internet was created with the goal of giving equal access to everyone. How do we close the digital divide? Or should we? "In fact, 50 percent of American households have Internet access, which is more than those that subscribe to a local daily newspaper," writes consultant Joe Celko. "Newspapers were supposed to be defenders of truth in a democracy, but nobody advocates a federally funded newspaper."[56]

THE INTERNET LIFESTYLE

Internet users have the convenience of shopping from their home or work desk. They can compare goods and vendors, chose an item, charge the purchase, and have it delivered to their home. They can sell unwanted items on eBay. This is the Internet lifestyle.

Travelers check the weather in Seattle. They access up-to-the-minute local, national, and even international news. They swap recipes, fashion tips, and gardening hints. This is the Internet lifestyle.

Adults keep in touch with friends and relatives around the world. Kids chat with schoolmates across town. Friends check their "buddy lists" to see which friends are currently online and

The Internet has undoubtedly altered social ties, but whether that's good or bad is a matter of contention. For those who are connected, communication has taken on many new forms, such as America Online's Instant Messaging and, as this grandmother and granddaughter demonstrate, videoconferencing.

say, "Hi, let's talk." People are using the Internet to extend their social network in a new way.

The technology of e-mail, online discussion, and on-demand information has fostered the creation and growth of online, or virtual, communities. Unlike face-to-face relationships with neighbors, coworkers, and classmates, these groups are not bound by geographic closeness. They are usually based on common interests, culture, or values. There are groups with members as diverse as rap musicians, breast cancer survivors, and maple syrup farmers. Some communities have defined rules, some charge fees, and some have entrance requirements. Many are very loosely organized and members come and go quite frequently.

These Internet facilities allow people to meet and converse with friends, join global communities, and exchange ideas freely, without censorship. Some people think this will lead to a more informed, engaged, and influential public. Others feel we will become a society of lonely ex-couch potatoes glued to impersonal computer screens. They point out that the Internet pulls people away from real-world interactions and their local community.

Anonymity is an important aspect of Internet communications. Some users suggest it softens social barriers. Shyness dissolves and people take risks; they make friends and perhaps find a mate. They are judged by what they say rather than being discriminated against because of their age, race, gender, or other

The Language of the Internet

In addition to changing the medium by which many people communicate, the Internet also altered the language we use in online social exchanges. Graphics were very limited in the early years of the Internet, so people developed symbols to express their emotions. Acronyms began to be used to convey information in a shorthand style.

EMOTICONS

Tilt your head to the left to read the emoticons.

:-)	happy
:-(	sad
;-)	wink
:-D	laughing
:-0	yelling
:-/	skeptical

ACRONYMNS

LOL	laughing out loud
ROTFL	rolling on the floor laughing
BTW	by the way
IMHO	in my humble opinion
FWIW	for what it's worth
FAQ	frequently asked question
HTH	hope this helps
TTYL	talk to you later
BFN	bye for now

physical characteristics. "Long live the Internet," one autistic user wrote, where "people can see the real me, not just how I interact superficially with other people." [57]

Sara Kiesler, a professor at the Human-Computer Interaction Institute at Carnegie Mellon University, says: "People will reveal more on-line than they might in person. Psychologically, economically and in every other way, it's cheap talk, people really enjoy it, and it feels safe too. You're just talking to the screen, sometimes people get oblivious to the dangers and they say things they wouldn't have said otherwise." [58]

Some people think the Internet is the perfect forum for discussing race issues. But Pulitzer Prize-winning author David Halberstam asks, "If you are speaking constantly anonymously, are you really speaking?" He continues, "Real conversation, it seems to me, is when two people who are different, and face each other, stumble with some kind of candor." [59]

In online debates of tough issues, the writers generally take on extreme positions. The discussions often end in anger and flaming, the sending of insulting or derogatory messages. No one has to compromise; they can just pull the plug on the conversation.

Others feel that online conversation lacks etiquette and truth. One problem is that a user can pretend to be any gender, race, occupation, or age. People can act out their fantasies or simply hide their true selves. They can become old or young, gay or straight, Jewish or Italian, doctor or teacher or rock singer.

In a study by psychologist Dr. David Greenfield, about 50 percent of those surveyed admitted that they'd lied online, mainly about their age, looks, weight, or marital status. Even kids admit to lying online. "I say I'm 17, in college and own a convertible," says a 14-year-old girl. "I'm 18 and six feet tall," says a 12-year-old boy. Another girl admits to teasing boys in chat rooms. "We flirt with boys, mess with their minds, then sign off abruptly," she says. [60]

Surveys probing the social consequences of the Internet differ in their conclusions. William Van Dusen Wishard, president of World Trends Research, noted that "researchers at Carnegie Mellon University cite a two-year study showing depression and loneliness appearing at greater levels in people using the Internet than in others not using it, or not using it as much. Extensive exposure to the wider world via the Net appears to make people less satisfied with their personal lives."[61]

A study conducted at Stanford University found that people who spend more time online spend less time with other human beings. Professor Norman H. Nie, coauthor of the study, said, "E-mail is a way to stay in touch, but you can't share a coffee or a beer with somebody on e-mail or give them a hug. The Internet could be the ultimate isolating technology that further reduces our participation in communities."[62] It might create a world numb to human emotion.

Social worker Janna Malamud Smith wonders if this is possible. "It seems that Professor Nie is assuming that hours with real human beings are an unqualified good thing. Call me a curmudgeon, but I often find them to be something of a mixed bag."[63] Smith would rather spend 15 minutes online doing her Christmas shopping than two hours driving from store to store, fighting for parking spots, and conversing with rude sales clerks.

Another finding of the Stanford report was that many people who are online five or more hours per week are spending less time watching television. Is that a bad thing? Smith does not think so; at least some of the communications are two-way.

David Mennahum and a group of technology writers assert: "Technology is making life more convenient and enjoyable, and many of us healthier, wealthier and wiser. But it is also affecting work, family, and the economy in unpredictable ways, introducing new forms of tension and distraction, and posing new threats to the cohesion of our physical communities."[64] Frederick L. McKissack Jr. quit his job in journalism and started working for an Internet development firm because he was scared. He says, "I began to have horrible dreams that sixteen-year-old punks were going to take over publishing in the next century

Some educators and social commentators worry that children are spending too much time in front of the computer and not enough with their family and friends. That loss of contact, they say, may affect the social fabric in unpredictable ways.

because they knew how to write good computer code. I'd have to answer to some kid with two earrings, who will make fun of me because I have one earring and didn't study computer science in my spare time." [65]

Author Clifford Stoll says he's met young nerds who can detail what's in their computer disk cache but have no idea when their family immigrated to the United States And he knows several high school students who use a word processor, but have never written a thank-you note. He says, "Kids that interact with computers rather than their parents miss out on the most important part of growing: being close to their families." [66]

The pope thinks that the Internet could diminish the desire for deeper thought and reflection. The pope also warns society about the worsening technology gap between rich and poor and says that true evangelization requires human contact, not just electronic relationships.

Sometimes electronic communication has enormous social value and potential. Jerry Berman, president of the Internet Education Foundation, points out that "September 11 made us acutely aware of what an important resource an open Internet played in making it possible for people, government, and policy leaders to connect with others, coordinate emergency response activities, reach and console loved ones, and spur charitable and cooperative activities."[67]

THE DIGITAL DIVIDE

When Web usage expanded in the early 1990s, Tim Berners-Lee, inventor of the Web, turned down opportunities to join booming businesses. Instead, he went to MIT and established the nonprofit World Wide Web Consortium. He says, "My motivation was to make sure that the Web became what I'd originally intended it to be—a universal medium for sharing information."[68]

A few years later, Berners-Lee was included in *Time* magazine's list of the "Most Important People of the 20th Century." His name was in the "Scientists and Thinkers" section along with those of Albert Einstein, Sigmund Freud, and Ludwig Wittgenstein. *Time* said that unlike other inventions that have moved the world, the World Wide Web was solely the work of one person—Berners-Lee. "He designed it. He loosed it on the world," wrote *Time*. "And he more than anyone else has fought to keep it open, nonproprietary and free."[69]

Although Berners-Lee tried to ensure equal access for everyone, studies in the 1990s showed that ethnic minorities, people in rural and poor areas, and the elderly were less likely to have access to the Internet, and therefore to the Web. Society was divided into the "haves" and "have-nots." This inequality of access to the Internet is referred to as the digital divide.

In April 2000, President Clinton announced his mission to open the digital frontier to all Americans "regardless of income, education, geography, disability or race." He said: "I want you to understand that while most people talk about the digital divide—

and it is real and it could get worse—I believe that the computer and the Internet give us a chance to move more people out of poverty more quickly than at any time in all of human history."[70]

Within months of Clinton's speech, studies showed that the digital divide was narrowing, and might actually vanish. Women, for example, had already closed the gap. In October 2000, Clinton released another statement saying that "many low-income, rural and minority households are beginning to 'get connected' at rates faster than the national average." He also said, "Access to these Information Age tools is becoming critical to full participation in America's economic, political and social life. Americans are using the Internet to vote, look for work, acquire new skills, and communicate with their children's teachers."[71]

Whereas in the United States access to the Internet has rapidly expanded, the rest of the world—with the exceptions of Scandinavia, Canada, and Australia—lags behind. A survey showed that 25 percent of Europeans had access, compared with 53 percent of Americans. The Internet has barely penetrated the developing world. In Bangladesh, for example, it would take up to eight years to save enough money just to buy a PC.

In the United States, schools and libraries provide public Internet access, but some observers say that home access opens up the true benefits of the Internet. "The way to spread computer ownership and Internet use is to make the technology better and cheaper," said American Enterprise Institute fellow and columnist James Glassman. "Only the private sector can do that—and it is. Today, you can buy a fabulous computer for less than $700. Unlimited connections to the Internet cost as little as $9.95 a month. No industry has improved its products as quickly or has pushed prices down as rapidly as the U.S. computer sector."[72]

As prices continue to drop, more and more people will connect to the Internet. Still, there will always be some digital divide because of those who live in poor regions and those who don't want to learn the new technology.

6

New Roles for Schools and Libraries

A 1996 report from the United States Advisory Council on the National Information Infrastructure stated: "In our Nation's classrooms, the Information Superhighway is being used to substantially improve the quality of general and technical education that our children receive."[73] On the Internet, teachers and students can take virtual field trips, perform science experiments, collaborate with students around the world, and conduct research.

Skeptics wonder if Internet access really helps education. Do teachers have the time to learn the new technology? Do students need social interaction more than virtual stimulation?

INTERNET-CONNECTED CLASSROOMS

Educators and students of all ages can now make use of computer-based learning activities that are available online through the Internet. These programs are especially effective in teaching math and science. Modeling and simulation help students see and understand basic concepts. For example, biology students can discover the laws of genetic inheritance using FlyLab. This website lets students "breed" fruit flies, formulate hypotheses, and run statistical procedures.

The Internet allows teachers to take students on field trips without worrying about transportation, chaperones, permission forms, fees, or the weather. The virtual field trip is not limited by place or time. In addition, the tours are interactive. Students can ask questions and exchange ideas with staff at the site they're visiting and with students from other schools.

Where can students go? Museums, libraries, schools, laboratories, foreign cities, and outer space. Classes might swim with sharks, visit the home of author Pearl Buck, spend a winter at Valley Forge, listen to frogs, travel through the human heart, tour a castle in Asia, or walk through Mr. Rogers's Neighborhood. Experts can "visit" a school without having to travel there.

Regardless of the school's wealth, size, or location, the Internet gives equal access to these field trips and to comprehensive library assets. School districts can offer courses in Chinese, calculus, and other subjects that might have a limited enrollment at one school. It also fosters communication among students with related interests.

School librarian Robert Koechley says, "Internet connections create interaction with the world outside the classroom which encourages a more relevant and exciting learning climate. The Internet is ideally suited to support a new paradigm in which the world becomes the 'whole village,' contributing to the education of the children." [74]

To help schools get connected, the Telecommunications Act of 1996 provided for a Universal Service Fund to give subsidies to schools and libraries. Schools can obtain discounts from 20 to 90 percent on telecommunications services, Internet access, and cabling in school buildings.

President Clinton and Vice President Al Gore supported NetDay, a nonprofit group of high-tech companies and individuals whose goal is to mobilize communities to connect classrooms to the Internet. These NetDays were dubbed "high-tech barn raisings" because businesses, governments, parents, students, and teachers join together to help wire classrooms for Internet use. At NetDay96, Clinton and Gore were at a high school in Concord, California, where they were part of an effort by 20,000 volunteers at about 3,000 schools in the state that installed 6 million feet of cable. Clinton said of the project, "Let the future begin."

Vice President Al Gore, left, and President Bill Clinton watch students using a computer at a high school in Concord, California, on March 9, 1996 — NetDay96. NetDay, a nonprofit group of high-tech companies and individuals, organizes businesses, government, and communities to connect their schools' classrooms to the Internet.

Michael Kaufman, one of the organizers of the California event, commented: "It's been interesting for us to watch because there's been so much written about how the electronic age is breaking up society, but this project is doing just the opposite."[75]

NetDay roused the state of California, and other communities followed suit. In 1994, only 35 percent of public schools were connected to the Internet, but by 1999, the number had risen to 95 percent. By 2001, it was almost 100 percent.

Skeptics wonder if the expense of the new technology is worth it. Wiring classrooms is not cheap, and the technology will be obsolete within perhaps ten years. Computers are also expensive and quickly become obsolete. In addition, they are targets of theft and hard to maintain.

Education student Chaitram Ramphal thinks the Internet will impair education. "One thing is for sure," he wrote, "the Internet threatens to push teachers into the sidelines and place itself as the heart of education. . . . But the replacement of teachers by the Internet will be an irreparable loss. Teachers teach the students how to behave in society. . . . Students need discipline and self-restraint to behave in a group. The school, functioning as a collection of individuals, teaches cohesion and responsibility. The Internet cannot teach these things."[76]

The kids have a different view. A study by the Pew Research Center found that 78 percent of youth of ages 12 to 17 who have Internet access say they believe the Internet helps them with schoolwork.

Over 40 percent of online teens say they use e-mail and instant messaging to contact teachers or classmates about schoolwork. However, the study did find one problem: 18 percent of online teens say they know of someone who has used the Internet to cheat on a paper or test.

Another concern is that students spend more time learning to use computer tools than learning concepts. Specific tools will quickly become obsolete; instead students need to learn skills such as how to retrieve information, recombine it, and use it to produce knowledge. What will also be needed in the near future is the capacity to learn throughout one's life since technology will continue to change rapidly.

Another criticism of the Web is that it creates poorly trained readers. Hypertext is associated with attention deficit disorder and a lack of scholarly authority. Critics charge that its structure encourages readers to merely skim the surface of a document, bypassing the deeper meaning within a text. But some books are meant to be skimmed, with only parts read more deeply; scientific, legal, travel, and cooking texts generally are not read cover to cover. Communications scholar Nancy Kaplan says hypertext might actually create better readers. "Whatever else we might observe about the process, it's certain that there's no automatic pilot for reading a hypertext," she says.[77]

The Internet has actually been a catalyst for reading, because it points users to other sources of information, including printed materials. Net sales of books have increased 7 percent annually; sales of juvenile books have risen over 13 percent. It seems that kids still find it more pleasing to curl up with a good book than to stare at a screen.

DISTANCE LEARNING

In the past, distance learning classes typically used postal mail, satellite television transmission, cable television viewing, and other media to extend the learning process beyond the walls of the school. Today, e-mail, the World Wide Web, and chat rooms provide an ideal environment for distance-learning classes. Courses are available anywhere, any time, and at all levels: high school, college, job training, and lifelong learning.

Gifted students often prefer online classes because they can progress more quickly. Students with physical disabilities sometimes prefer not to travel to school. Students in remote areas can avoid long bus rides by attending class online. Other students prefer distance learning to avoid peer pressure or violence on campus.

A small number of online secondary schools have been established in the United States. Choice 2000 is a public charter school in Riverside, California, that offers grades 7 through 12 online via the Web. It claims to be the first completely online public high school in the United States. The programs are accredited by the Western Association of Schools and Colleges.

Students must provide their own computer and are expected to log on every day, Monday through Friday. Classes are held at specific times and presented in a live chat room format. The school also offers extracurricular activities such as dances, field trips, and picnics so students can interact face-to-face.

Why do students and parents pick Choice 2000? The school's website states: "We have medically fragile students, highly gifted, hyperactive students who had difficulty in a regular classroom. We have students who are fearful of the conditions in large public schools, and those who have gotten in trouble there. Our program, that leads to a high school diploma and preparation for advanced schooling, offers an opportunity to all, from the convenience and safety of their home." [78]

Colleges and universities are rushing to offer online education, too. "The Internet will probably be the single most democratizing force in education," said Columbia Business School Dean Meyer Feldberg. [79] At present, distance learning is not in the mainstream of campus life; it is used principally by part-time students who cannot easily travel to campus due to work or parenting duties, are interested in noncredit classes, or are seeking special courses.

The University of Phoenix (*http://online.phoenix.edu*) was one of the first accredited universities to offer complete degree programs online. In 2001, it was the largest online institution, with 6,000 students. The school's philosophy is "you can earn your degree via the Internet whenever and wherever you want— at home in the evenings, at work during lunch, or while traveling on business. No commuting. No lines. No wasted effort. You just click into class and start learning." [80]

The University of Phoenix Online offers undergraduate and graduate degrees in such areas as e-business, management, marketing, information systems, and nursing. Students simply need a computer and an Internet service provider. They retrieve lectures, questions, and assignments from their instructor and then review them offline when and where it is most convenient for them. Students also have access to online research libraries and services, as well as other successful professionals with whom they can share ideas, debate issues, and get and give advice.

One concern about distance learning is that parents and students might choose distance learning instead of traditional schools to escape from opposing religious, cultural, or other beliefs. Schools should not fall into the trap of customizing the curriculum to the wishes of parents and students. Instruction should provide a view of things from another perspective; encountering differences is part of the education mission.

"The Internet can probably deliver all the information taught in a university, as can a good encyclopedia. So why go to college?" asks Clifford Stoll in *Silicon Snake Oil*. "Because isolated facts don't make an education. Meaning doesn't come from data alone. Creative problem solving depends on context, interrelationships, and experience. The surrounding matrix may be more important than the individual lumps of information. And only human beings can teach the connections between things."[81]

THE CYBER-LIBRARY

As more and more information is made available online, there might be less reason to maintain a physical library. It is possible that the entire library system is at risk of extinction. But Stoll doesn't think so. He writes, "this bookless library is a dream, a hallucination of online addicts, network neophytes, and library-automation insiders."[82]

Stoll says that many people don't realize that the information that's online is pretty much limited to works produced over the last 15 years or so. "Nothing's been digitized before 1980. Well, almost nothing," he says.[83] The online Project Gutenberg has scanned hundreds of books for downloading from the Web. Works like *Moby Dick*, the Bible, *Alice's Adventures in Wonderland*, and *Romeo and Juliet* are available. More titles are added every month, but still, it is far from being the online, bookless library that some people advocate.

One hurdle for the digital library is the difficulty of putting books online. New books are protected by copyright laws and cannot be reproduced. Old books require scanning, which is tedious and time-consuming. The situation is the same for newspaper and magazine articles.

Although some people predict that information on the Web will be so widely available that brick-and-mortar libraries will be unnecessary, others point to the fact that little material published before the computer revolution is in a digital format. In addition, many users who don't have a computer at home access the Internet at their local library, as these two men are doing at Philadelphia's Public Library.

While libraries have not become bookless, they are choosing to acquire some documents on CD-ROM or via the Internet. Should a library continue to get paper copies of magazines and newspapers that are available online? Paper journals have subscription fees, handling and cataloguing expenses, shelf space requirements, and theft problems. Should the library store archived copies or pay for access to archival databases on the Web? How will they serve people who do not want to use the Internet or those who cannot use it because of physical or mental disabilities? Librarians have to carefully weigh the media options.

The Internet certainly is one way to expand the walls of the library. It gives patrons access to previously unavailable information and allows the card catalog to be viewed from any computer with an Internet connection.

Project Gutenberg

Project Gutenberg began in 1971 when there was extra computer time available on a mainframe at the University of Illinois. Operators were given an account with $100,000,000 of computer time in it. The operators were encouraged to do whatever they wanted with that fortune in their "spare time" in the hope they would increase their job proficiency.

Michael Hart, one of the operators, decided there was nothing he could do that would be worthy of the cost of that much computer time. So he decided to create $100,000,000 worth of value in some other manner. Less than two hours later, he announced that the greatest value created by computers would not be computing, but would be the storage, retrieval, and searching of what was stored in our libraries.

He typed in the text of the Declaration of Independence and tried to send it to everyone on the networks. The administrators of those networks were not happy about being bombarded by the document, so they persuaded him to stop. Next, he posted the first electronic text to the networks, and Project Gutenberg was born. Hart felt that he had earned the $100,000,000 because a copy of the Declaration of Independence would eventually be downloaded and become an electronic fixture in the computer libraries of 100,000,000 of the computer users of the future.

Hart enlisted the help of hundreds of volunteers who supported his idea of putting lots of famous and important texts online to make them freely available to everyone in the world. Project Gutenberg (*http://promo.net.pg*) is now over 30 years old. As of November 2002, it contained the text of 6,267 books.

At this time, there is no evidence that use of the Internet is affecting the frequency with which people use libraries. A study conducted during the spring of 2000 found that more than 75 percent of Internet users also used the library. Instead of the Internet eliminating the library, as Stoll claimed, it actually seems to be enhancing it. Citizens who come to the library to access the Internet or attend Internet user group meetings sometimes become more vocal supporters of the library.

Librarians have a large role in the Internet environment. In fact, they were among the first users of the Internet, and advocated expanding access to it. A book published by the American Library Association (ALA) states: "While corporate giants and politicians discuss how to cut up the electronic pie, legions of America's librarians are serving that pie to the nation's information hungry." [84]

Library professionals are not abandoning books; rather they are applying their years of experience in information management to the cyber world. Access, expression, and responsibility are issues that librarians wrestled with long before the invention of the Internet.

While librarians are now spending time patrolling the Internet and monitoring users, they are also educating people about this new information resource. They teach patrons how to use search engines and how to evaluate the credibility of what they find. A tendency to be lazy might make people accept the first answer they find to a question and never wonder whether the answer is accurate, but Internet users need to learn how to discriminate between different sources. According to the ALA, "the skills of librarians in evaluating and processing information and in acting as intelligent agents are more valuable than ever before in this new medium." [85]

7

Health Matters

AT ISSUE

To avoid shopping in public, 19-year-old tennis star Serena Williams started shopping online. "Next thing I know, it's fun and I was addicted," she says.[86] She spent as many as six hours a day online buying clothes, shoes, and things for her dog. But she kicked the habit and no longer spends so much time online.

"It is important that we recognize the addictive power of the Internet," says Dr. Kimberly Young, a clinical psychologist and director of the Center for On-Line Addiction (COLA). "High profile individuals such as Serena are drawn to the anonymity that cyberspace affords."[87]

Other health professionals contend that Internet addiction is a fake disease that is being treated with fake medicine. Some people spend too much time reading, watching television, and working, but TV addiction, book addiction, and work addiction are not being suggested as legitimate mental disorders.

TOO MUCH INTERNET

The Internet can be entertaining, educational, and social. Some users may even experience a high from it, but excessive Internet use may result in health concerns. Sitting for hour after hour surfing the Internet limits physical activity. Users become "mouse potatoes," and that can lead to physical problems such as headaches, back and neck pain, wrist ailments, or obesity. A concern of some health professionals is that spending too much time online can begin to interfere with a person's social relationships or even lead to Internet addiction.

Computer users may broaden not only their intellectual horizons on the Internet, but also the kinds of pain and illnesses they experience. Excessive use can restrict healthy exercise and cause musculoskeletal problems. One of those problems is carpal tunnel syndrome, a repetitive motion injury that causes numbness and pain in the affected hand.

A 1996 study conducted by Kimberly Young for the University of Pittsburgh reported that there was a widespread problem: 396 out of 496 users were dependent on the Internet. Young founded the Center for On-Line Addiction, the first treatment clinic and training institute specializing in cyberspace-related disorders, including cybersex addiction, cyberaffairs, problem day trading, compulsive online shopping and gambling, and childhood Internet addiction.

However, not all health professionals agree with Young's study methods or her conclusions. Dr. Mark Griffiths, a psychologist at Nottingham Trent University, thinks Young's criteria were too wide-ranging and classified too many people as Internet addicts. "A lot of these people aren't addicted to the Internet—they're addicted to sex or gambling and they use the Internet as a tool." He continued, "You can't classify an addiction in terms of its medium—if someone's addicted to gambling and spends all their time in a betting shop, we don't say they're addicted to betting shops."[88]

In a more recent study conducted by Oliver Seemann of Ludwig-Maximilians University Psychiatric Clinic in Munich, Germany, it was found that only 20 of 809 people fulfilled the criteria for an addiction syndrome, such as withdrawal symptoms, increasing tolerance, and loss of control. Experts estimate that only about 2 or 3 percent of all Web users are "Internet addicts"—individuals who typically neglect family and friends, lie about how much time they spend online, and mold their daily lives to fit their Internet use.

Many health authorities believe this so-called Internet addiction actually just taps into a preexisting condition, such as an addiction to gambling or a sense of isolation and depression. Maressa Hecht Orzack, a clinical psychologist at Harvard Medical School, says all of her patients with Internet addiction have at least one other problem. "Depression, social phobia, impulse control disorder, and attention deficit disorder are commonest," she says. But there is no single pattern related to the Internet. "Some [people] use it for excitement or a new sense of identity; some to reduce tension; some for companionship; others, most tellingly, because it's a place where they belong. Typically they are lonely people."[89]

New users, online less than one year, are more likely to be

excessive users. These newcomers seem to immerse themselves in the Internet for a time. For example, a study about online chat activity found that, at first, people were enchanted by the activity. Disillusionment and a decline in usage followed this period. Later, a balance was reached where the level of chat activity normalized.

Problematic Internet use can occur in any age, social, educational, or economic group. "The visual thing is the biggie," says psychologist Dr. David Greenfield. Exchanging e-mail or chatting is like getting "love letters, but the words can be even more powerful than words on paper, because when people stare at a screen, they experience a trancelike dissociative quality, a hypnotic effect." He says that when you add color, movement, sound, endless availability you have a combination that's very "potent and seductive."[90]

Internet overuse has real dangers. People lose their jobs because they spend too much time online, either failing to show up for work or misusing their computer at work. By 1996, some companies had installed monitoring devices to track Internet usage by employees. One company discovered that only 23 percent of their employees' Internet usage was business related. This type of online procrastination, called "cyberslacking," results in significant losses in productivity.

"The debate over the existence of Internet addiction will probably continue for some time," says Marshall University psychology professor Keith W. Beard. "Regardless of whether or not the term *Internet addiction* is used, there are people who are developing a harmful dependence on the Internet and need assistance in addressing this problem."[91]

Interventions for overuse of the Internet can take many different forms. Medication can be used to help the individual cope with the anxiety or depression that could be a factor in excessive use. Classical conditioning techniques may focus on breaking the associations made between originally neutral stimuli (the computer and the Internet) and the cue that automatically prompts the addictive response. Cognitive therapy techniques could be used to help with irrational beliefs and triggers to engage in addictive behavior. Intervention could also focus on resolving social difficulties that may contribute to the individual hiding behind the computer.

Most experts say that the preferred treatment includes a combination of therapy and participation in self-help recovery groups. Some counselors believe in controlled Internet use, some do not. Some believe that once the Internet has become a problem, the risks of exposure outweigh the need for access.

A 17-year-old in Renton, Washington, was coming home from school and going online so she would not miss out on any socializing. She especially enjoyed instant messaging, but she felt rejected when people did not immediately respond to her messages. Her parents became concerned as she grew more and more depressed. With the help of a psychologist, the young lady broke her habit by not using the instant messenger and taking an antidepressant.

Many experts tell patients with Internet-related compulsive disorders to avoid computers. Those who can't feasibly function without the Internet should move the computer to a public area of their home or workplace, have a cyber chaperone who monitors their online activity, install blocking software programs, and go online only when they have a specific reason to do so and then log off as soon as that task is completed.

ONLINE HEALTH CARE

Some health professionals say that the Internet can be used to provide health information and care. For example, Kimberly Young has found that Internet addicts are not receptive to the idea of 12-step recovery groups; she uses online counseling. Young says that when COLA first opened, "I quickly became the Ann Landers of online therapists." [92] She charges $75 an hour for treating a patient via the computer.

Not all counselors think that kind of treatment is ethical. They think a therapist and patient need to talk in an office or at least on the telephone. One counselor commented, "In addition to being ethically questionable, I don't think it is particularly effective to treat patients with the very tool through which they are dissociating."[93]

While the Internet may or may not be useful in the treatment of addicts, it can be useful in other treatments. In an article in the *American Medical News,* Lynne Lamberg asserts that online groups are a useful service. They "give participants both practical information and the comforting realization that they are not alone in facing their disease or disability."[94]

She says online self-help groups can also "help people maintain their health, speed recovery and boost their odds of improvement, according to studies done in the 1990s of patients with breast cancer, asthma, diabetes, arthritis and other diseases."[95] Medical care costs may be reduced, too, because patients in self-help groups bring problems to their physicians at an earlier stage and visit emergency rooms less often.

Through the use of voice synthesizers and other devices, people who may not be able to see or to type can participate in these groups. So can people who might be isolated because they live in remote places, lack transportation, are disabled, or have a fear of leaving their home.

As of 1999, AOL reported that about 1,000 messages a day were being posted in its health and medical forum. About 73 million people in the United States have gone online to research prescription drugs, prepare for a visit to a doctor, explore new ways to lose weight, or perform other health-related searches. One reason people go online is to find information quickly, but they should be sure to take time to examine the credibility of websites. The Public Citizen Health Research Group says that much of the medical information online is wrong, misleading, or even dangerous.

A 1997 study focused on information about fever in children. Only 4 of 41 Web pages adhered closely to the recommended pediatric guidelines for this ailment. Worse yet, several of the sites suggested treatments that are known to place a child at high risk of coma or death without warning of this risk. The study concluded: "The Internet contains a wealth of health-related information, but this research clearly shows that using these types of web pages to diagnose and treat illnesses is like playing Russian roulette."[96]

The Internet can be a useful tool, especially for people like Sigrid Cerf, the wife of Internet pioneer Vint Cerf. Sigrid lost almost all of her hearing at the age of 3, and for 50 years she wore an amplification device. Using the Internet, the couple researched an experimental electronic inner ear implant. Sigrid located people who had the implants and contacted a specialist at Johns Hopkins University by e-mail. She had the implant and "she and I talk[ed] to each other on the phone for the first time in thirty-one years," recalls Vint Cerf.[97]

Many health professionals are looking for ways to use the Internet to provide better care for their patients. Health-care providers are harnessing the Internet's power for everything from direct patient communications to sophisticated strategies for managing patients at home.

An Illinois health organization, First Health Group Corp., plans to reimburse physicians for Internet consultations. At this time, the service is available only for chronic-care patients. "Patients with chronic conditions tend to benefit most from regular physician contact to catch early signs of potentially acute episodes. Online communication is an effective way for these patients to communicate with their physicians to catch these early warning signs," said the medical director for First Health.[98]

The online medical hub Medem hosts websites for 83,000 physicians, and in 2002, it launched a new service to convince physicians to consult with patients via the Internet. About 8,000 physicians signed up for the new secure messaging service. Patients can log onto a physician's site, enter payment information, and send a request. Physicians set their own rates for the online sessions and may override the charge for simple things like appointment requests, prescription requests, or follow-up questions.

Communicating with patients via the Internet is providing the healthcare community with new flexibility in monitoring chronic problems. Here, diabetic Bill Parks of Augusta, Georgia, checks in with home health nurse Debbie Durham (on the computer screen), who remotely measures his blood pressure and pulse.

For patients with life-threatening conditions and life-altering diagnoses, Cleveland Clinic now provides specialist consultations and second opinions via the Internet. "More and more patients are taking responsibility for their health, and they are looking for access to quality medical decisions in emergency situations as quickly as possible," says the e-clinic's executive director.[99] The Internet can remove the barriers of where and when medical services are provided.

8

Continuing Expansion

AT ISSUE

The Internet has already transformed society. Our businesses, health care systems, schools, libraries, and government have changed. But the Internet continues to change, too; that is part of its architecture. It is constantly being expanded to handle more users and more traffic. What will the Internet look like in five years? Ten years?

"In the short term, the impact of new technologies like the Internet will be less than the hype would suggest," says Paul Saffo, director of the Institute for the Future. "But in the long term, it will be vastly larger than we can imagine today." [100]

MORE TRAFFIC, MORE BANDWIDTH

The common wisdom applied in the computer industry is Moore's Law, named in honor of Gordon Moore, cofounder of Intel. Moore's Law holds that computing power will double every 18 months. According to some experts, bandwidth (the capacity for Internet traffic) will do the same, but maybe even more rapidly.

Larry Roberts, director at ARPA from 1967 to 1973, interviewed Internet carriers to determine current traffic figures. "We have added our numbers onto the old ARPA and NSF statistics, and it shows that growth has been steady since the inception of the Internet," said Roberts in January 2002. "Traffic has more than doubled every year." [101]

Roberts predicts that this trend will continue until the end of the decade. After that, he says, Internet traffic may start to slow. For now, the big problem is a lack of superfast connections.

The Internet is a network of networks connected by "pipes." Pipes go into our homes and offices, our universities and government facilities. Big pipes connect smaller pipes. If any of those pipes become clogged, the system slows down.

As Web pages grow to contain more graphic, video, and audio elements, they increase astronomically in the amount of data that must be transmitted. At the same time, more and more users are accessing the Internet. Many analysts believe we are headed for lots of congested pipes.

In his book *Web Rules,* Tom Murphy proposes three solutions: don't increase the total amount of data on the Internet, prioritize Web usage, or build more bandwidth. The first solution is implausible because there is no way to keep people off the Internet or to limit multimedia features. Charging for high priority, or fast response, would be difficult to implement and goes against the underlying values of the Internet. Installing bigger pipes— in other words, using broadband connections—seems the most viable solution.

Broadband is a means of transmitting data at a higher band-width, or carrying capacity. The greater the bandwidth is, the more efficient and faster the network is. The old phone lines that carry Internet service to many houses today are not broadband, but there are a variety of broadband services.

Digital subscriber line (DSL) service sends high-speed Internet service over unused frequencies available on standard telephone wire. Fiber optic cables are thin fibers of glass that carry light signals rather than electrical pulses. Internet2 is a coalition of universities and businesses aimed at creating a separate Internet that increases Web access speeds by up to 1,000 times using fiber-optic lines.

Cable modems and wireless-based Internet access are other broadband delivery systems. For rural citizens, two-way satellite service may be an option. Another new technology is a Wi-Fi

Fiber optic cables that carry broadband signals are speeding data transmission rates by 1,000 times over the rate of standard telephone lines. Signals travel through these cables as light rather than electrical pulses.

network. The connection hangs in the air as a radio signal and communicates with a wireless router and wireless cards in the PC. The signal can be used anywhere within 30 feet of the transmitter, allowing neighbors and nearby drivers with laptops and wireless network software to piggyback on the network.

Other equipment will have to keep up with the increased bandwidth. Network routers and switches and users' PCs will have to work faster. How long will it take to install the equipment? How much will it cost?

UNDERRATED OR OVERSTATED?

The Internet delivers communications in a way unimaginable at the turn of the twentieth century. Computing power and publishing power have been put in the hands of large populations. The Internet gives people a feeling of empowerment, and that feeling will spread to other parts of their lives.

"The secret is that the Internet doesn't actually *do* much; it's a powerful tool for people to use," says Esther Dyson of EFF. "It's not something worth having, but it's a powerful lever for people to use to accomplish their own goals in collaboration with other people. It's more than a source of information; it's a way for people to organize themselves." [102]

One popular image of the Internet is that it's a fantastic collection of thriving communities, where people who are dispersed geographically can meet, work together, and make the world a better place. But another image depicts it as grim and unhealthy, with weird people, perverts, criminals, and mad bombers lurking anonymously—an alienated and alienating place.

"The Internet has been blamed for decreased productivity in the workplace, decreased family time, strains in relationships, perpetuation of false information, and the development or exacerbation of psychological problems," writes journalist Keith Beard. [103] It is portrayed as a medium used to find potential victims of fraud and child abuse, to discover secrets about friends, and to plot terrorism.

Writer Barry Golson observes: "Following the pop of the dot-com bubble, the Internet swung from glory to folly faster than any phenomenon in my lifetime. It took 10 years for perceptions of the Vietnam War to change to lost cause from gung-ho; with the Internet, it took six months." [104]

Improvements in computer equipment must accompany the improvements in transmission speed afforded by fiber optic cables. This external modem from Zoom Telephonics supports the higher upload speeds required for faster Web browsing.

The Internet seemed shrouded in a dark cloud in November 2001, when Golson wrote those words. But the statistics showed a different story. Internet traffic had quadrupled in the previous 12 months. Also, with new high-speed connections, users spent twice as much time online. Was the Internet being underhyped?

Robert Kahn, coinventor of TCP/IP, says, "All great inventions take years to be explored and appreciated." He thinks creative uses of wireless Internet hold great promise for the future. For example, a device might pinpoint your location and lead you to the nearest restroom, diner, hospital, or police station. "The age of this technology has only just begun," says Kahn. "It's tip of the iceberg now." [105]

As the Internet grows and changes, it will bring excitement and uncertainty. "I imagine one could say: 'Why don't you leave me alone? I want no part of your Internet, of your technological civilization, of your network society! I just want to live my life!'" writes Manuel Castells, professor of sociology at the University of California, Berkeley. "Well, if this is your position, I have bad news for you. If you do not care about the networks, the networks will care about you, anyway. For as long as you want to live in society, at this time and in this place, you will have to deal with the network society. Because we live in the Internet Galaxy." [106]

How people adapt to the Internet and how the Internet is adapted for society remains to be seen. Tim Berners-Lee, creator of the World Wide Web says, "The experience of seeing the Web take off by the grassroots effort of thousands gives me tremendous hope that if we have the individual will, we can collectively make of our world what we want." [107]

1957 The Soviet Union launches *Sputnik I*, the first artificial satellite to orbit Earth.

1958 The U.S. Department of Defense forms Advanced Research Projects Agency (ARPA).

1962 Paul Baran of the Rand Corporation conducts study on packet-switching networks.

1963 ARPA employee J.C.R. Licklider writes memo addressing "Members of the Intergalactic Computer Network."

1968 ARPA awards contract for Interface Message Processors (IMPs) to Bolt, Beranek, and Newman; Douglas Engelbart invents hypertext.

1969 First node (host system) of ARPANET installed at UCLA; second node installed at Stanford Research Institute; third node installed at University of California, Santa Barbara; fourth node installed at University of Utah.

1971 ARPANET has 15 nodes.

1972 First basic e-mail programs written; specifications for FTP written.

1973 First international connections made to ARPANET.

1974 TCP/IP outlined in a paper by Robert Kahn and Vinton Cerf.

1977 ARPANET has over 100 nodes.

1981 ARPANET has 213 nodes.

1983 ARPANET begins to use TCP/IP, and thus the Internet is born; ARPANET has 562 nodes; MILNET is formed to take military networks off ARPANET.

1984 ARPANET/Internet has over 1,000 nodes.

1985 National Science Foundation (NSF) organizes NSFNET backbone to connect five supercomputers.

1986 ARPANET/Internet has 5,000 nodes.

1988 First time a worm halts Internet traffic.

1989 ARPANET/Internet has 100,000 nodes; ARPANET is shut down. America Online offers online services, but no connection to the Internet.

1990 Tim Berners-Lee creates the World Wide Web.

1991 Gopher invented at University of Minnesota; the Internet Society (ISOC) is founded.

1992 World Wide Web goes public; amendment made to NSF Act to allow commerce on the Internet; 1 million hosts are on the Internet.

1993	Web browser Mosaic is released; Web grows by 341,000 percent in one year.
1994	Netscape Communications introduces new Web browser, called Navigator.
1995	NSFNET reverts back to research network; Internet service providers handle U.S. backbone traffic; Amazon.com sells its first book.
1997	Yahoo! goes public.
1998	The eBay website goes online.
2000	Napster goes online; AOL agrees to buy Time Warner for $165 billion.
2001	The dot-com bubble bursts and over 500 Internet-based companies go out of business; over 400 million Internet users worldwide.
2002	Internet2 has 200 university, 60 corporate, and 40 affiliate members.
2003	Over 35 million web servers on the Internet.

1 Douglas Rushkoff, "The People's Net," *Yahoo! Internet Life,* July 2001.

2 Quoted in Norman H. Nie and Lutz Erbing, *Internet and Society: A Preliminary Report.* Stanford, Calif.: Stanford Institute for the Quantitative Study of Society, February 17, 2000.

3 Nie, *Internet and Society.*

4 Janet Abbate, *Inventing the Internet.* Cambridge, Mass.: MIT Press, 1999, 2.

5 Brendan P. Kehoe, "Preface," *Zen and the Art of the Internet,* January 1992. <*http://www.cs.indiana.edu/ docproject/zen/zen-1.0_toc.html*>

6 "Pope Says Internet a New Opportunity to Evangelize, but Warns of Dangers of Instant Gratification and Loss of Values," *AP Worldstream,* January 22, 2002.

7 Manuel Castells, *The Internet Galaxy.* Oxford, England: Oxford University Press, 2001, 3.

8 Quoted in Richard T. Griffiths, *History of the Internet, Internet for Historians (and Just About Everyone Else).* <*http://www.let.leidenuniv.nl/ history/ivh/chap2.htm*>

9 Peter Jennings and Todd Brewster, *The Century for Young People.* New York: Doubleday, 1999, 236.

10 Andrew L. Shapiro, *The Control Revolution.* New York: Century Foundation, 1999, xiii.

11 Quoted in Joe Flower, "The Future of the Internet: An Overview," in *The Future of the Internet,* edited by Charles P. Cozic. San Diego, Calif.: Greenhaven Press, 1997, 17.

12 Peter H. Salus, *Casting the Net.* Reading, Mass.: Addison-Wesley, 1995, vii.

13 Quoted in Stephen Segaller, *Nerds 2.0.1.* New York: TV Books, 1998, 37.

14 Quoted in Segaller, *Nerds,* 29.

15 Quoted in Matt Friedman, "Internet 'Historians' Need to Get Facts Straight." *Computing Canada,* November 29, 1999, 26.

16 Quoted in Segaller, *Nerd,* 71.

17 Quoted in Abbate, *Inventing the Internet,* 142–143.

18 Salus, *Casting the Net,* 216.

19 Quoted in George Beekman, *Computer Confluence: Exploring Tomorrow's Technology.* Upper Saddle River, N.J.: Prentice-Hall, 2001, 263.

20 Quoted in Katie Hafner and Matthew Lyon, *Where Wizards Stay Up Late.* New York: Simon and Schuster, 1996, 186.

21 Tim Berners-Lee, *Weaving the Web.* San Francisco: Harper San Francisco, 1999, 162.

22 Rushkoff, "The People's Net."

23 Rushkoff, "The People's Net."

24 Jaron Lanier, "Taking Stock," *Wired.com,* January 1998.

25 U.S. Department of Justice Antitrust Division. <*http://www.usdoj.gov/atr/ cases/f2600/iii-b.pdf*>

26 Quoted in Flower, "The Future of the Internet," 15–16.

27 Rushkoff, "The People's Net."

28 Quoted in "Cerf's Up," *Director,* May 2001, 89.

29 Wired Digital, Encyclopedia of the New Economy. <*http://hotwired.lycos.com/ special/ene*>

30 Quoted in Segaller, *Nerds,* 342.

31 J. Neil Weintraut, "Introduction," in *Architects of the Web,* by Robert H. Reid. New York: John Wiley & Sons, 1997, xxxvii.

32 Quoted in Carter Henderson, "How the Internet Is Changing Our Lives," *Futurist,* July/August 2001, 38.

33 Shapiro, *The Control Revolution,* 54.

34 Quoted in *The Internet,* edited by Gray Young. New York: H.W. Wilson, 1998, 63.

35 Quoted in Henderson, "How the Internet Is Changing Our Lives," 38.

36 Nanette Byrnes and Paul C. Judge, "Internet Anxiety," *Business Week Online,* June 28, 1999.

37 Rushkoff, "The People's Net."

38 Quoted in Shapiro, *The Control Revolution,* 48.

39 Quoted in David Streitfeld, "Internet Retailers Will Revert to Traditional Methods of Commerce," in *The Internet: Opposing Viewpoints,* edited by Helen Cothran. San Diego, Calif.: Greenhaven Press, 2002, 187.

40 Rushkoff, "The People's Net."

41 Quoted in Reid Goldsborough, "Making Money on the Web, Now the Old-Fashioned Way," *New Orleans City Business,* July 8, 2002.

42 Quoted in Dan Egbert, "Internet Companies Change Policies, Increase Fees to Improve Business," *The News & Observer,* April 25, 2002.

43 The 2002 State New Economy Index, "Introduction." *<http://www.new-economyindex.org/states/2002/introduction.html>*

44 Quoted in Kirstin Downey Grimsley, "Telecommuting Rewires Traditional Views of the Workplace," *Washington Post,* August 31, 2002, E1.

45 Bill Lessard and Steve Baldwin, *NetSlaves: True Tales of Working the Web.* New York: McGraw-Hill, 2000, 245.

46 Statement by the President. June 26, 1996. *<http://www.epic.org/cda/clinton_cda_decision.html>*

47 The Electronic Frontier Foundation, "Introduction." *<http://www.eff.org/EFFdocs/about_eff.html>*

48 Quoted in Paul Freiberger and Michael Swaine, *Fire in the Valley.* New York: McGraw-Hill, 2000, 429.

49 Quoted in Willie Schatz, "Operation: SunDevil," *The Washington Post,* Business Section, May 31, 1990.

50 Christos J. P. Moschovitis, Hilary Poole, Tami Schuyler, and Theresa M. Senft, *History of the Internet.* Santa Barbara, Calif.: ABC-CLIO, 1999, 124.

51 Quoted in Fred T. Hofstetter, *Internet Literacy.* Boston: Irwin/McGraw-Hill, 1998, 21.

52 Quoted in Moschovitis, *History of the Internet,* 207.

53 Gail Robinson, "From Geek to Glamour in 30 Years," *New Statesman,* July 10, 2000.

54 Quoted in Young, *The Internet,* 68.

55 Quoted in *The Economist,* "Copyright Infringement May Increase on the Internet," in *The Future of the Internet,* edited by Cozic, 99.

56 Joe Celko, "PC Promises: A PC on Every Desk and a Chicken in Every Pot," *Intelligent Enterprise,* November 15, 2002.

57 Shapiro, *Control Revolution,* 48.

58 Quoted in Amy Harmon, "On-Line Trail to an Off-Line Killing," *The New York Times,* April 30, 1998, A1.

59 Quoted in "Internet Anonymity Fosters Stark Dialogue About Race," *The New York Times,* March 8, 1998, 26.

60 Quoted in Young, *The Internet,* 114.

61 Quoted in Henderson, *Futurist.*

62 Quoted in Nie, *Internet and Society.*

63 Janna Malamud Smith, "Online but Not Antisocial," *The New York Times,* February 18, 2000.

64 Quoted in *The Internet: Opposing Viewpoints,* edited by Cothran, 13.

65 Frederick L. McKissack Jr., "Cyberghetto: Blacks Are Falling through the Net," in *The Internet,* edited by Young, 98.

66 Clifford Stoll, *Silicon Snake Oil .* New York: Doubleday, 1995, 59.

67 Quoted in "Internet 9.11 Reviews the Value of the Internet as a Resource During Tragedies on September 11, 2001," *U.S. Newswire,* September 3, 2002.

68 Berners-Lee, *Weaving the Web,* 84.

69 Quoted in J. Mark Lytle, "Great Thinkers: Einstein, Freud and . . . Berners-Lee," J@pan Inc., May 2002.

70 U.S. Department of State, *"Excerpts from Remarks by the President at Digital Divide Kick-Off,"* April 4, 2000. *<http://usinfo.state.gov/usa/blackhis/divide3.htm>*

71 Quoted in "Commerce Secretary Mineta Releases Report Finding Progress on Digital Inclusion," *Commerce News,* October 16, 2000. *<http://www.ntia.doc.gov/ntiahome/press/2000/fttn101600.htm>*

72 James Glassman, "A Right to an Internet Connection?" *American Enterprise,* April/May 2000.

73 U.S. Advisory Council on the National Information Infrastructure, "The Information Superhighway Will Offer Many Benefits," in *The Future of the Internet,* edited by Cozic, 20.

74 Robert Koechley, *Libraries and the Internet* (Fort Atkinson, Wis.: Highsmith Press, 1997), 41.

75 Quoted in Janet Kornblum and Rose Aguilar, *"Clinton, Gore Kick Off NetDay96,"* CNET News.com, March 10, 1996.

76 Chaitram Ramphal, "The Internet Will Impair Education," in *The Future of the Internet,* edited by Cozic, 77.

77 Quoted in Moschovitis, *History of the Internet,* 166.

78 Choice 2000, *"General Information."* *<http://www.choice2000.org/geninfo.html>*

79 Quoted in Henderson, *"How the Internet Is Changing Our Lives."*

80 Online College and University and
Degree Program Online, "*University
of Phoenix*." <*http://www.online-
college-and-university.com/phoenix-
university.html*>

81 Stoll, *Silicon Snake Oil*, 134.

82 Stoll, *Silicon Snake Oil*, 176.

83 Stoll, *Silicon Snake Oil*, 175.

84 Edward J. Valauskas and Nancy R.
John, *The Internet Initiative*
(Chicago: American Library
Association, 1995), vii.

85 Valauskas, *Internet Initiative*, xiv.

86 Quoted in "*Serena Williams: 'I Wasn't
Able To Stop*,'" ESPN.com, August 9, 2001.

87 Quoted in "*Serena Williams Is
Not Alone—Many High Profile
Individuals Hooked on the Internet*,"
netaddiction.com, August 20, 2001.

88 Quoted in "*Internet Addicts 'Need
Help*,'" BBC News, September 29, 1999.
<*http://news.bbc.co.uk/1/hi/health/
460208.stm*>

89 Quoted in Peter Mitchell, "*Internet
Addiction: Genuine Diagnosis or Not?*"
Lancet, February 19, 2000.

90 Quoted in Rose Pike, "*Log On, Tune
In, Drop Out*," ABCNews.com,
March 26, 1999.
<*http://abcnews.go.com/sections/living/
DailyNews/netaddiction032699.html*>

91 Keith W. Beard, "*Internet Addiction:
Current Status and Implications for
Employees*," Journal of Employment
Counseling, March 2002, 9.

92 Quoted in Brian McCormick,
"*Internet Addiction: Hooked on the
Net*," amednews.com, June 19, 2000.

93 Quoted in McCormick, "*Internet
Addiction*."

94 Lynne Lamberg, "*Internet Self-Help
Groups Can Improve Health Care*," in
The Internet: Opposing Viewpoints,
edited by Cothran, 99.

95 Lamberg, "*Internet Self-Help
Groups*."

96 Public Citizen Health Research
Group, "Medical Information on the
Internet Undermines Health Care,"
in *The Internet: Opposing Viewpoints*,
edited by Cothran, 107.

97 Quoted in Segaller, Nerds, 359–360.

98 Quoted in "PPO to Reimburse for
E-Mail Consultations," *Family Practice
Management*, September 2000, 24.

99 Quoted in Dave Carpenter,
"Treatment on the Net," *H&HN:
Hospitals & Health Networks*,
February 2002, 26.

100 Quoted in Beekman, *Computer
Confluence*, 289.

101 Quoted in "Internet Founder Says
His Invention Still Alive," *Xinhua
News Agency*, January 17, 2002.

102 Esther Dyson, *Release 2.0, A Design
for Living in the Digital Age*, New
York: Broadway Books, 1997, p. 35.

103 Beard, "*Internet Addiction*."

104 Barry Golson, "A Bubble of Bad
News Hides True Web Reality,"
Advertising Age, November 5, 2001.

105 Quoted in Shannon Henry, "What
Will Internet's Next Era Bring?"
Toronto Star, May 27, 2002.

106 Castells, *The Internet Galaxy*, 282.

107 Berners-Lee, *Weaving the Web*, 209.

BOOKS

Abbate, Janet. *Inventing the Internet.* Cambridge, Mass.: MIT Press, 1999.

Berners-Lee, Tim. *Weaving the Web.* San Francisco: Harper San Francisco, 1999.

Castells, Manuel. *The Internet Galaxy.* New York: Oxford University Press, 2001.

Cothran, Helen, ed. *The Internet: Opposing Viewpoints.* San Diego, Calif.: Greenhaven Press, 2002.

Cozic, Charles P., ed. *The Future of the Internet.* San Diego, Calif.: Greenhaven Press, 1997.

Dyson, Esther. *Release 2.0: A Design for Living in the Digital Age.* New York: Broadway, 1997.

Freiberger, Paul, and Michael Swaine. *Fire in the Valley.* New York: McGraw-Hill, 2000.

French, Laura. *Internet Pioneers.* Berkeley Heights, N.J.: Enslow, 2001.

Gaines, Ann. *Tim Berners-Lee and the Development of the World Wide Web.* Bear, Del.: Mitchell Lane, 2002.

Gates, Bill. *The Road Ahead.* New York: Viking, 1995.

Hafner, Katie, and Matthew Lyon. *Where Wizards Stay Up Late.* New York: Simon and Schuster, 1996.

Hofstetter, Fred T. *Internet Literacy.* Boston: Irwin/McGraw-Hill, 1998.

Lessard, Bill, and Steve Baldwin. *NetSlaves: True Tales of Working the Web.* New York: McGraw-Hill, 2000.

Lewis, Michael. *Next, the Future Just Happened.* New York: W.W. Norton, 2001.

Moore, Dinty W. *The Emperor's Virtual Clothes.* Chapel Hill, N.C.: Algonquin Books, 1995.

Moschovitis, Christos J.P., Hilary Poole, Tami Schuyler, and Theresa M. Senft. *History of the Internet.* Santa Barbara, Calif.: ABC-CLIO, 1999.

Murphy, Tom. *Web Rules.* Chicago: Dearborn Financial, 2000.

Nie, Norman H., and Lutz Erbring. *Internet and Society: A Preliminary Report.* Stanford Institute for the Quantitative Study of Society: February 17, 2000.

Ojeda, Auriana, ed. *Technology and Society: Opposing Viewpoints.* San Diego, Calif.: Greenhaven Press, 2002.

Reid, Robert H. *Architects of the Web.* New York: John Wiley & Sons, 1997.

Salus, Peter H. *Casting the Net.* Reading, Mass.: Addison-Wesley, 1995.

Segaller, Stephen. *Nerds 2.0.1.* New York: TV Books, 1998.

Shapiro, Andrew L. *The Control Revolution.* New York: Century Foundation, 1999.

Slevin, James S. *The Internet and Society.* Cambridge, England: Polity Press, 2000.

Spector, Robert. *Amazon.com: Get Big Fast.* New York: HarperBusiness, 2000.

Sunstein, Cass. *Republic.com.* Princeton, N.J.: Princeton University Press, 2001.

Waldrop, M. Mitchell. *The Dream Machine.* New York: Viking, 2001.

Young, Gray, ed. *The Internet.* New York: H.W. Wilson, 1998.

PERIODICALS

Beard, Kevin. "Internet Addiction: Current Status." *Journal of Employment Counseling,* March 2002.

Golson, Barry. "A Bubble of Bad News Hides True Web Reality." *Advertising Age,* November 5, 2001.

Henderson, Carter. "How the Internet Is Changing Our Lives." *Futurist,* July/August 2001.

Rushkoff, Douglas. "The People's Net." *Yahoo! Internet Life,* July 2001.

"Pope says Internet a New Opportunity to Evangelize, but Warns of Dangers of Instant Gratification and Loss of Values." *AP Worldstream,* January 22, 2002.

WEBSITES

Amazon.com
http://www.amazon.com

America Online
http://www.aol.com

Center for Online and Internet Addiction
http://www.netaddiction.com

Electronic Frontier Foundation
http://www.eff.org

Microsoft
http://www.microsoft.com

New Economy Index
http://www.neweconomyindex.org

Technews.com
http://www.technews.com

Wired
http://www.wired.com

Zen and the Art of the Internet
http://www.cs.indiana.edu/docproject/zen/zen-1.0_toc.html

FURTHER READING

Berners-Lee, Tim. *Weaving the Web.* San Francisco: Harper San Francisco, 1999.

Freiberger, Paul, and Michael Swaine. *Fire in the Valley.* New York: McGraw-Hill, 2000.

Gates, Bill. *The Road Ahead.* New York: Viking, 1995.

Hafner, Katie, and Matthew Lyon. *Where Wizards Stay Up Late.* New York: Simon and Schuster, 1996.

Moschovitis, Christos J.P., Hilary Poole, Tami Schuyler, and Theresa M. Senft. *History of the Internet.* Santa Barbara, Calif.: ABC-CLIO, 1999.

Reid, Robert H. *Architects of the Web.* New York: John Wiley & Sons, 1997.

Salus, Peter H. *Casting the Net.* Reading, Mass.: Addison-Wesley, 1995.

Segaller, Stephen. *Nerds 2.0.1.* New York: TV Books, 1998.

Spector, Robert. *Amazon.com: Get Big Fast.* New York: HarperBusiness, 2000.

Young, Gray, ed. *The Internet.* New York: H.W. Wilson, 1998.

WEBSITES

Internet Society
http://www.isoc.org

PBS's Nerds 2.0.1
http://www.pbs.org/opb/nerds2.0.1

World Wide Web Consortium
http://www.w3c.org

Hobbes' Internet Timeline
http://www.zakon.org/robert/internet/timeline

Sandra Weber has an M.B.A. from Temple University and a B.S. in mathematics and computer science from Clarkson University. She is a veteran netizen, having started using the Internet in 1993. She has worked as a technical writer and quality assurance analyst in the computer industry and as an instructor of computer science at Montgomery County Community College in Pennsylvania. She developed and taught a course about the Internet in 1996. The next year she taught the class via the Internet as a Web-based distance-learning course. She is now devoted full-time to writing books and magazine articles.

DATE DUE